Kenneth Lo is the foremost expert on Chinese cuisine writing and broadcasting in English. Born in Foochow, China, in 1913, he studied physics at Peking University and then English Literature at Cambridge and London. He has pursued a variety of careers during his time in Britain, as a diplomat, a fine-art publisher, an industrial relations and welfare officer for Chinese seamen, a journalist, a lecturer, and a professional tennis player. He is best known, however, for his many authoritative books on Chinese cooking and eating. He has contributed articles and columns to innumerable journals and magazines, and has appeared many times on television. The Grafton edition of his *Cooking the Chinese Way* has been successfully in print for twenty-five years. Now in his seventies, Kenneth Lo is still extremely active and productive, and this he attributes to the fact that he follows his own advice – about cooking and eating the Chinese way.

By the same author

Chinese Cooking Encyclopaedia
Chinese Food
Chinese Vegetable and Vegetarian Cooking
Cooking the Chinese Way
Peking Cooking
Quick and Easy Chinese Cooking
Cheap Chow
Chinese Provincial Cooking
Chinese Cooking and Eating for Health
Cooking and Eating the Chinese Way
More Wok Cookery

KENNETH LO

The Wok Cookbook

GRAFTON BOOKS

A Division of the Collins Publishing Group

LONDON GLASGOW
TORONTO SYDNEY AUCKLAND

Grafton Books
A Division of the Collins Publishing Group
8 Grafton Street, London W1X 3LA

First published in Great Britain by Grafton Books 1981
Reprinted 1981 (three times), 1982 (six times),
1983 (three times), 1984 (three times), 1985 (three times),
1986 (twice), 1988 (twice)

Copyright © Kenneth Lo 1981

ISBN 0-583-12929-3

Printed and bound in Great Britain by
Cox & Wyman Ltd, Reading

Set in Times Roman

Contents

The Wok

The wok is simply a round-bottomed frying-pan. But because of its shape, its depth and the dome-shaped cover, it can be put to many more uses than just frying, shallow-frying or stir-frying. It is used in China for steaming, braising, as a double-cooker as well as for stir-frying, shallow-frying and deep-frying.

1. A Wok with lid and stand.

Deep-frying is, in fact, seldom used in domestic kitchens in China (only in restaurants) if only because of the cost of the large quantities of oil required. Foods which are deep-fried in the west are usually shallow-fried in China. In shallow-frying a moderate amount of oil is heated in the 'well' of the wok and swilled around to grease a large surface area of the pan. Foods which require frying are dropped or lowered into the well piece by piece and pushed to the sides whilst other pieces are introduced. When all the pieces of food have been initially fried then they can all be turned around in the wok with a perforated spoon. Thus a comparatively small amount of oil (125-250 ml or ¼-½ pint) can perform the function of a western deep-fryer which often requires a larger quantity of oil to start with.

In stir-frying, only a very small amount of oil is required – perhaps no more than 2-3 tablespoons – even if you are cooking 3-4 average portions of food. Much of the cooking and heating is achieved by the heat from the metal of the pan. To use too much oil would make the dish too greasy, although we Chinese are more conscious and deliberate in the use of 'flavoured oil' for flavouring than westerners. Stir-frying, where foods are cut small before cooking commences, has, of course, the great advantage of saving cooking time as well as the other very important element of being able to produce an immense range of 'mixed' dishes. Because this form of cooking is almost 'instant', stir-frying is also often called 'quick-frying' or 'quick stir-frying'.

The wok is regularly used in China for 'steaming'. This is done in the wok by placing the food or foods to be cooked in a heat-proof dish or bowl and then placing the latter on top of a rack (such as a cake rack) standing in boiling or simmering water. The dish or bowl containing the food should have its rim at least 7.5 cm (3 in) above the surface of the water so that the foods do not become awash with water during the cooking. Steaming in the wok can be 'short' or 'long'. 'Short steaming' is employed in the cooking of fish, seafoods or tender meat and should last from a few minutes to no more than 10-15 minutes. 'Long steaming' can be a very lengthy affair of more than 2-3 hours. 'Long steaming' in the wok is, in effect, using the wok as a double-cooker for tough cheap cuts of meat.

'Braising' is a process used in Chinese cooking as a prolongation of stir-frying. It is used to extend the cooking when the 'instant' nature of stir-frying is insufficient to tenderize the foods. It is done by simply adding some liquid into the wok and lowering ·the heat. The addition of the liquid should prevent the foods from burning and lengthens the cooking time from 3-4 minutes or less to 10-15 minutes or more and should help to tenderize the foods. Once the liquid in the wok has largely evaporated, some small adjustments in seasoning are effected and aromatizing agents (sesame oil, wine or liqueur) are added for a last moment of stir-frying before serving.

'Shallow-frying' as practised in China is a process very akin to the western way of frying bread. It is a comparatively static form of frying using only a small amount of oil or fat. The purpose of 'shallow-frying' is to cook and crispen the food which may or may not have been cooked previously in some other way: dumplings (previously steamed), stuffed vegetables, mushrooms, aubergines or cucumbers are often cooked in this way, whether under cover or open (many smoked dishes such as Chinese 'smoked fish' are usually shallow-fried for a few minutes before serving).

Another cooking process for which the wok is eminently useful is what can only be described as an extension of stir-frying: the process of simply tossing hot foods or ingredients together, which is akin to that of making 'hot salads'. Once again, in such a form of cooking only a very small amount of oil or fat is used – mainly to prevent foods from sticking to the pan (such as rice or noodles which are tossed with vegetables, shrimps, prawns, or diced meats which have previously been cooked). This is not the formal process of stir-frying. Nevertheless, it is a form of cooking which is often practised in Chinese cooking when bulk foods have to be tossed and mixed with savoury foods. For this type of cooking, the wok, because of its shape and capacity, is extremely suitable.

That the wok can be used for cooking familiar western dishes is illustrated by twenty-odd recipes of typical British, American or French dishes which can be easily and conveniently cooked in the wok (in the Chinese fashion!).

CLEANING THE WOK

Although woks, these days, are sometimes made of stainless steel, copper or aluminium, the bulk of them are still made in the age-old traditional Chinese way, with beaten iron. In this latter form, it would rust easily if it were simply washed in water and left to dry. It should be thoroughly dried and rubbed with some grease before storing away. Otherwise, the wok is a tough piece of utensil which can be subjected to an enormous amount of work and handling; this could immediately be confirmed if you could see how a Chinese chef uses it in a restaurant kitchen. Immediately after a dish is cooked and dished out, he places the wok under a running tap and gives it a clean with a bamboo brush and a wipe and the wok is immediately pushed on top of a gas flame again to cook the next dish. Because the wok is still burning hot when washed, a Chinese cook would seldom resort to the use of any detergent (in any case, the continual use of detergents is a western addiction which we Chinese have not grown into).

In restaurant cooking, the cook would seldom bother to grease the wok as it is often used more than 200 times a day and each time it is used it is greased with oil or fat by the cooking itself. It can be said that a wok in the Chinese kitchen is always 'shining in use' and hardly has the chance of 'rusting in idleness'. In the western kitchen where it may not be in continual use it should be greased lightly after washing (which can be done with a little detergent, but preferably just under hot running water) and rubbed dry with a clean cloth.

Wok Cookery

Chinese systems and concepts usually favour the round to the angular. Even in martial arts, many of the movements are circular – as against the 'straight from the shoulder' of English gentlemen – and in philosophical thinking the Chinese are more inclined to think round (towards perfection in smoothness of relations) than to allow their minds to act like a laser beam probing and penetrating in a straight line into the unknown of the universe. It is from these movements and relations that the Chinese have distilled whatever understanding and wisdom they may have evolved and possess. The shape of the wok with its round contours, suitable for stirring, turning and tossing, must have, itself, derived from this roundness of notion and background.

Another of the ingrained Chinese concepts or ideas is the one of speed – the movement should be like lightning as in swordsmanship where you should aim to decapitate the enemy three times before he could bring his heavy axe into position to deliver his first mighty (headless) blow! Because of the wok's round contours, it makes the stirring, turning, gathering and scooping of foods and ingredients much easier, faster, and more natural than in a conventional flat-bottomed frying-pan.

The word 'instant' here should convey an entirely different connotation from that of the current expression 'instant food'. For the Chinese use of the word 'instant' should not only denote speed but also freshness and care and precision of preparation so that all the natural flavour of food will arrive on the table unimpaired, and, if anything, further enhanced. It is this love and care and precision in preparation which produces good-quality Chinese food – for, indeed, they are the essential ingredients in the production of any foods of the highest standards.

When the wok first came into play and eventually into general use is unrecorded. It probably came into its own through an evolutionary process and came to be accepted as an established cooking utensil in the Chinese kitchen in mid-antiquity (in late Han or Tang-Sung Dynasties) when the burning of wood and charcoal in standard stoves became a well-established practice. Before that, many Chinese cooking utensils made of iron, bronze, or earthenware were much heavier, and were probably made (some with legs) to stand over an open fire (or bonfire) rather than to be used on top of well-shaped stoves or cookers.

As compared with these earlier implements, the wok is definitely of much lighter construction. It can usually be handled with one hand. Indeed, as a utensil, it is light even when compared to many similar pieces of equipment in a modern kitchen. Because of the current fashion of having frying-pans which are both large and heavy to convey the appearance of being both rustic and professional, we have come to accept these unwieldy pieces as if we are all cooking ten-portion paellas every day. To be useful, the wok should be large but light.

The wok should be big so that not only a great quantity of food can be cooked but also small amounts, since in both cases, all the foodstuffs in it will slide and gravitate towards the central part of the bottom. It should also be large because it is much less likely to spill and splash when you are turning and tossing vigorously as in stir-frying. This is even more important in shallow-frying or deep-frying when a very much larger quantity of hot oil is being employed and spilling could be disastrous. Finally, it is useful to have a large wok because it can then double as a steamer. This is especially important when steaming fish, which straddles the whole width of the wok, so it will have to be of at least 37-45 cm (15-18 in) in diameter to accommodate a whole fish of any dimension. Besides, it will require quite a sizeable wok to generate the necessary volume of steam when cooking several steamed dishes at once in several layers of basket-steamers placed one on top of the other over the wok. Hence, in a Chinese domestic kitchen there is usually a very large wok, with a multi-storeyed basket-steamer sitting on top of it which appears to be emitting steam all the time. Although on the top layer some dishes may only be there to keep hot, at the bottom layer, nearest to the boiling water, several other dishes are being vigorously steamed.

2. Steam baskets piled up in a wok.

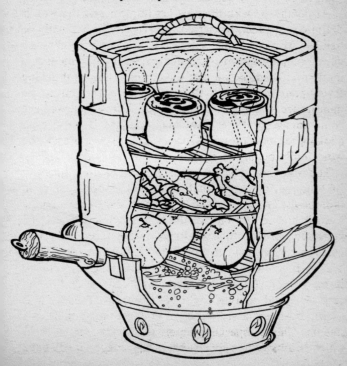

With these considerations in mind, let us take a closer look at what exactly takes place in the several typical methods which are employed by the Chinese when cooking in a wok and what they aim to achieve.

QUICK STIR-FRYING

'Quick stir-frying' as a method of cooking has often been described in Chinese cookbooks. I shall describe it here again in its particular relation to the wok, since the latter is a utensil which appears to be specially designed for stir-frying. In stir-frying what is needed is speed of cooking and consequently 'instant heat'. By 'instant' I mean the ability to turn the heat up instantly when required, as well as to turn it down equally instantly and remove it altogether when not required. This can only be achieved if the utensil is lightweight so that the heat can be conducted through the metal onto the food materials at the touch of a finger. And conversely, what is also important is that once the wok is taken off the heat (or if the heat is shut off) it should start to cool immediately; there should be no retention of heat in the metal which would cause the food materials in it to continue to cook quite vigorously for some time after the wok has been removed from the source of heat. Hence, the wok must not be very thick or heavy but must be tough enough to withstand a fair amount of stirring, scraping and tossing.

3. Some cutting techniques.

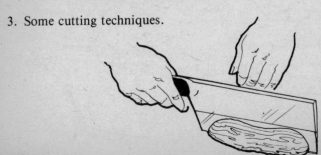

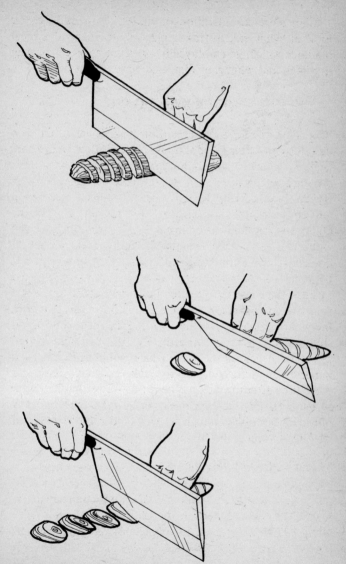

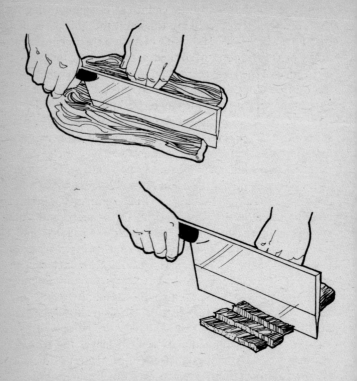

Quick stir-frying is particularly suitable for cooking very
fresh foods whether meat, fish, seafood or vegetables. The
technique is to cut the food material into wafer-thin slices
or dice it into small cubes (about the size of small sugar-
lumps) and cook them in an instant over high heat in a
small amount of oil. This high-heat high-speed cooking
not only causes the food material to become instantly
sealed and well-cooked on the outside (in about ½-1½
minutes) but because of the thinness of the materials and
the high temperature of the oil and the metal with which it
is in close contact, the heat penetrates the food from all
sides, causing the juice in the meat or vegetable to come to

an instant boil but with little chance of escaping owing to the shortness of the cooking time and the quickly sealed exterior of the food. The result of such a treatment is that every piece of food so cooked should be 'bouncy' and extra juicy. When the main food material has reached this stage of cooking, it is immediately given a short rest, by either removing it from the pan or pushing it to the sides or one end of it, away from the centre of heat, whilst a selection of seasonings, sauces and supplementary materials are added into the centre of the wok for a moment's cooking and 'concocting' into an 'instant sauce'. At this point, the main material is returned to the centre of the wok for a few final moments' stirring, combining and blending with the sauce and the supplementary materials. The result is usually quite delicious and delectable. What this short process achieves is to combine the fresh juiciness of good food materials in all their own characteristic flavours with the savoury deliciousness of the sauce which has been individually and newly concocted. In order to be able to savour all the fine qualities of such a dish it will have to be served and consumed almost immediately after it leaves the wok. If you can start off with good fresh food materials there is hardly any form of cooking to beat quick stir-frying.

Steaming During Stir-frying
A short period of steaming is a process which is often used in conjunction with stir-frying. It quite often happens that after the main food material (meat etc.) has been initially stir-fried and either removed from the centre of heat or put aside temporarily before being returned for the final mixing with the sauce, some of the supplementary materials (frequently vegetables such as cauliflower, broccoli, beans, cabbage, zucchini etc.) which have been introduced into the wok require longer cooking to tenderize them than can be achieved by a moment's stir-frying, even

at high heat. What is normally done in these circumstances is that a small amount of boiling water, stock or wine (or a mixture of them) is added to the wok and a lid is placed firmly over it. The latter forms a dome under which the liquid is converted into steam, helping the food materials to become tender without burning or charring. This process does not usually take longer than 3-5 minutes to achieve its purpose – often less – and then the lid is removed and the main materials which have had some preliminary cooking are re-introduced into the wok for the final stirring together.

Final Glossing or Aromatizing

After the process of 'instant steaming' as referred to above, foods, especially vegetables which have a high percentage of water, often require 'glossing' just before serving. This is achieved in Chinese cooking by adding a small amount of fat – usually melted lard – to turn and stir with the hot vegetables for a few seconds before dishing out. This has the effect of enriching the vegetables and making them taste more succulent. An aromatic effect can often be achieved at the same time by adding a few drops of sesame oil and a couple of teaspoons of finely-chopped chives or spring onions.

In the case of meat cooking, the same 'glossing' effect is achieved by adding a mixture consisting of 2-3 teaspoons of cornflour blended with 2-3 tablespoons of water or stock. The 'aromatizing' effect can be achieved at the same time by the addition of 2-3 tablespoons of wine or liqueur or 1-1½ teaspoons of sesame oil into the wok before finally stirring it all together. If chopped garlic is to be added, whether to a meat or vegetable dish, it should be added for a few moments' stir-frying with the main food material before the addition of the liquid. This is also the point where adjustments to seasonings can be made if necessary. Since all meats contain a certain percentage of fat, no further fat will need to be added at this juncture as is often done in vegetable cookery.

SHORT-TERM BRAISING

Braising is usually a long-term process of low-heat cooking aimed at tenderizing food materials. In stir-frying, there are sometimes cases where the main food material or materials which are being cooked require somewhat longer cooking to tenderize than just quick stir-frying or even short-term steaming (ie when the meat is tough and not of the ideal quality). In such instances, the food material or materials will have to be subjected to a period of slow-heat cooking (of 15-30 minutes) with a slight addition of water, stock or wine (or a mixture of them all plus seasoning sauces to vary or intensify flavour) and the cooking should be carried on either with or without a cover. In cases where some reduction is desired, no cover should be applied. It is normal to resume the process of stir-frying with final 'glossing' and 'aromatizing' after a period of short-term braising. Where a winey flavour is desirable, a period of braising in wine can be recommended with meats such as pork, chicken, lamb or veal (but not beef, which requires much longer cooking to tenderize than just 20-30 minutes of braising) if they are not of the best cuts. But if they are, the instant quick stir-frying is still the most recommended way to cook them.

In the case of vegetables which are somewhat tough, a short period of braising in meat stock with soya sauce and a touch of wine to be followed by a final 'glossing' and 'aromatizing' would generally make them most palatable and appealing.

All these processes of short-term braising, 'glossing', and 'aromatizing' are related methods to the central method of quick stir-frying.

STEAMING

The one method which is not related to stir-frying is steaming, a method which is widely employed in Chinese cooking, especially in home cooking. There are two types of steaming used in China:

Short Steaming

Foods which are of good quality and are very fresh (all fish and seafoods must fall into this category or they should not be used) can be 'short steamed'. When cooking in a wok, this is achieved by placing the food materials (pre-seasoned and dressed) in a heat-proof dish or bowl which is then placed on a rack inside the wok, and covered with a dome-shaped lid. Tin foil can be placed loosely over the food to prevent condensed water from the lid dripping into it. A good, continual blast of steam is generated when the water at the bottom of the wok (which should be about a quarter to a third full of water) is brought to a vigorous boil. As there should be a minimum of 750 ml-1 litre (1½-2 pints) of water in the wok, it will have to be a large one. The water can be easily replenished simply by pouring boiling water down the side of the wok, as it should be of a slightly larger circumference than the basket-steamers which are stood or placed inside it. This vigorous, short-blast steaming usually lasts for no more than 8-12 minutes for foods which have been cut into thin slices or diced into small cubes. But when cooking a whole fish, which can be more than 5 cm (2 in) thick in places, the steaming will often have to be extended to 20 minutes in order to assure that no part of it is undercooked. As a rule, however, in using steaming as a method of cooking, the actual process of heating or steaming should be kept, as in stir-frying, as short as possible. It is by the shortness of the process that the sweet, fresh, flavoursome juices of the food can be best retained. In Chinese fish cookery, 'glossing' with hot melted fat is often employed to good effect towards the end, to enrich the dish.

For people who are used to the ways of Chinese cooking – ie stir-frying where the majority of food materials and ingredients are turned and mixed up together – it is a relief to use a method (steaming) where the foods and ingredients used in a dish will come out as neatly as they were when first put into the wok – without their being 'messed up' during the process of cooking ('messing up' is a state of affairs which should be strenuously avoided wherever possible in Chinese cooking). Besides, in steaming the dishes can usually be brought to the table clouded in steam, which makes them appear more appealing. This form of short-steaming is called in China 'Ch'eng' which carries a connotation of 'purity'. All fresh foods of fine quality should be cooked and presented as 'purely' as possible and the wok is often employed to this purpose, as a steamer.

Long Steaming

Long steaming differs from short steaming, in that the foods are not subjected to the direct action of the steam. They are placed in a heat-proof bowl or receptacle where the top is closed with a lid, greaseproof paper, or tin foil (tied firmly on) and steamed steadily for a long period of time (1 hour to 5-6 hours). When used in a wok, the closed receptacle or bowl is placed on a rack situated 2.5-5 cm (1-3 in) or so above the boiling water and the wok is covered with a dome-like lid. The boiling water will, of course, have to be constantly replenished and the level checked at regular intervals as the cooking progresses. However, as the boiling and steaming are not kept up at a great pace it will only be necessary to replenish the water once every half an hour (as against four times an hour in vigorous steaming). Such prolonged cooking at a steady temperature is usually able to render or reduce foods to extremes of tenderness, hence many cheaper cuts of meat (or tougher and older poultry items) can be cooked to a great advantage in this manner, since such cuts of meat (ie shin beef, mutton, trotters, hand of pork etc.) are intrinsically more flavoursome than the younger and tender meats. Many Chinese dishes which in western jargon are best called 'meat puddings' are usually cooked in this manner. Another advantage of such long-term cooking is that the 'flavour construction' of the dish can be built up at leisure with the use of pickles, dried foods, herbs, wine etc., in addition to the usual flavourings and seasonings. This form of steaming is styled 'T'ung' in China.

THE POSSIBLE USE OF THE WOK IN WESTERN COOKING

Because of the afore-mentioned capabilities of the wok, there is no doubt that many workaday western dishes can also be cooked in it to advantage, especially those which require speedy cooking as well as those which entail the blending and mixing of food materials and ingredients. The use of the wok in the western kitchen will certainly, to some degree, influence the whole western approach to the treatment of food in cooking. For instance, everybody makes salads in the west. Once the wok is put into use in the kitchen, many will start making 'hot salads' by tossing vegetables in the wok with oil, soya sauce, vinegar and a touch of other seasonings and sesame oil. The many Victorian savoury 'pudding' dishes, which one seldom comes across these days, can, of course, be cooked in the wok in the same manner as the Chinese 'T'ung' dishes, by steaming for a good length of time.

On the other hand, in 'Cuisine Nouvelle' or 'Cuisine Minceur' which are nowadays so much in fashion, the

'Ch'eng' form of quick-steaming can certainly be applied to the cooking of many fresh food dishes, such as fish, seafoods, vegetables and the more tender meat cuts.

However, the area of cooking where Chinese ways are most likely to have the maximum impact if the wok is introduced into the kitchen is, of course, in quick stir-frying. This form of cooking should become extremely popular because it is easy, because it is speedy and because by mixing foods and ingredients together a great many dishes can be created. In this world of mundane routines, everyone has a strong desire, if only a latent one, to be creative. It may be that the introduction of the wok into the western kitchen may precipitate a culinary revolution by releasing untold, untapped creative energy all across the land.

In the concluding chapter of this book, we shall make some experiments in cooking some typical or established western dishes in the wok the Chinese way to trigger this 'revolution'. The reader can then, through experiments, judge for himself or herself whether the wok has a practical use or beneficial influence. The verdict on the dishes will be in the eating!

Quick Stir-fried Dishes

I shall start with 'quick stir-frying' as this is the form of cooking where the maximum number of dishes can be produced (through the variation in blending of ingredients and cross-cooking of different types of food materials) and where, from the practical point of view, there is actual saving of time and effort in the preparation of a meal. What is extremely attractive in stir-frying for the newcomer is that he or she is able to achieve 'instant' results; a simple meal of 2-3 dishes can be prepared and served in 20-30 minutes (and with practice in even less time).

To achieve these quick results, one should bear in mind that the best of Chinese cooking is often very simple (as Escoffier said of French cooking: 'Fait simple!'). Many people who have not entered into the realm of Chinese cooking are often burdened with the thought that in Chinese cooking you will need a lot of exotic spices. My advice is to forget the spices. To cook effectively in the Chinese way all you need are the three strong-tasting vegetables: spring onions (or scallions), garlic and root-ginger. The only types of flavourings required are soya sauce, soya paste (or yellow bean sauce or hoisin sauce) which are all easily obtainable from any Chinese food store. The other seasonings and flavourings you will need are the common things which you would find in any kitchen: salt, pepper, mustard, chilli sauce, vinegar, tomato puree, wine (or sherry), chicken stock cubes and oil.

With these few things, which one can purchase for not much more than a pound, one can go immediately into action. At the moment of writing the wok is still an inexpensive piece of equipment. It might be useful to have two of them, as it could be an advantage to cook a dish in two woks at the same time; one for cooking the meat and the other for cooking the rice, noodles or vegetables and then finally using one of them to assemble them in. As I have previously mentioned, one should, at all cost, avoid 'messing things up' in Chinese cooking; by keeping materials and ingredients apart and cooking them separately in the early stages, one has less chance of falling into a messy situation. If one lacks a second wok one can always use an ordinary frying-pan in place of it.

In the preparation of a Chinese meal one should aim to serve at least two dishes at the same time. Since two dishes are the minimum, one should be a bulk dish: *Fried Rice* or *Fried Noodles* to be served with one stir-fried savoury meat dish. It is only when you are preparing more than one meat or savoury dish (fish, seafood etc.) that one would serve plain boiled or steamed rice with them. In order to achieve a better balance, if you already have two savoury meat dishes to serve with plain rice and you are adding a third, that should be a pure vegetable dish. In Chinese food one is always striving for the best balance – not only because of health but because a well-balanced meal is both visually more attractive and more enjoyable to consume.

In the first section of the book, under 'Quick Stir-Fry Cooking', I shall aim at the preparation of a simple meal which will consist of one stir-fried meat dish with Fried Rice or Fried Noodles. (Please do not get the impression that in these 'fried' foods one is using and consuming quantities of oil or fat; in fact, in relation to the total quantity of foods consumed, one is using not much more oil or fat than one would use on properly buttered toast.) These meals are aimed at serving 2-3 people with average or better-than-average appetites.

These meals can be augmented to serve 3-4 people,

simply by adding a pure vegetable dish to the 2-dish combinations.

Since in these 'combinations' of dishes, the Fried Rice and Fried Noodles are the 'constants' we shall proceed here to prepare these dishes first in the wok.

FRIED RICE AND FRIED NOODLES

Basic Fried Rice (for 2-3)

- 1 medium onion
- 2-3 rashers of bacon
- ½ tsp salt
- 2-3 eggs
- 2½ tbs vegetable oil
- 300-400 g (¾-1 lb) boiled rice (in China leftover rice is normally used)
- 1½ tbs butter or lard
- 2-3 tbs green peas
- 1-1½ tbs soya sauce

Preparation
Cut onion into thin slices, bacon into matchstick shreds. Add salt to eggs, and beat with fork in a cup or bowl for 10 seconds.

Cooking
Heat oil in a wok over medium heat. When hot add onion and bacon. Stir-fry them together for 1½ mins. Push them to one side of the wok and pour the egg into the oil. When somewhat set, stir them together with the onion and bacon. When the eggs have set, add the rice. Break up all the lumpy bits and mix them evenly with the egg, onion and bacon. After 1½ minutes' turning and mixing together, remove the wok from heat and put aside temporarily. Heat butter or lard in a separate frying-pan or wok. When it has all melted add the peas. Stir them over medium or high

heat for 1¼ mins and pour them evenly over the rice etc. in the wok. Return the wok to the heat, sprinkle the contents with soya sauce. Turn and stir for 1 more min and serve.

Serving

Divide the Fried Rice into 2-3 bowls for the 2-3 diners at the table. To be consumed with one meat/savoury dish.

Basic Fried Noodles (or Chow Mein) (for 2-3)

    3-4 stalks spring onion
    3 rashers of bacon (or 100-200 g (¼-½ lb) lean and fat
      pork)
    1-2 sticks celery
    100 g (¼ lb) mushrooms
    400 g (1 lb) spaghetti or noodles
    2½ tbs vegetable oil
    1½ tbs soya sauce
    2 tbs butter or lard
    ½ chicken stock cube (dissolved in 3-4 tbs boiling water)
    1 tbs dry sherry

Preparation

Cut spring onions into 2-5 cm (1 in) sections (after removing roots and discoloured leaves). Cut bacon or pork into matchstick shreds after removing rind. Cut celery and mushrooms into 4-5 cm (1½-2 in) large shreds, after removing roots or stalks. Boil spaghetti for 18 mins or noodles for 8 mins and drain.

Cooking

Heat oil at the bottom of a wok. When hot add bacon or pork, and stir them around in the hot oil for 1½ mins over medium heat. Add spring onions and stir continuously for 1 further min (until much of the fat from the bacon has melted into the oil). Pour in 1 tbs soya sauce. Stir once, and pour in the spaghetti or noodles to mix with the bacon and spring onions. Stir, turn and mix well. Leave the contents to cook over low heat.

Meanwhile, heat butter or lard (or a mixture of the two) in a small frying-pan or wok. When hot add mushrooms and celery. Increase heat to high. Stir the contents around for 1½ mins. Pour in the stock and ½ tbs soya sauce. Continue to stir and turn over high heat for 1½ mins. Pour the contents over the noodles in the wok. Turn and mix them together for 30 seconds. Sprinkle the noodles with sherry and serve.

Serving

Divide the contents into 2-3 bowls (any leftovers should be kept in the wok for 'seconds' where it can be heated up again instantly when required). The dish should be eaten with at least one meat/savoury dish, unless one is in a particularly impecunious state – when the noodles and vegetable contents of the dish could be increased by 50% and the dish would be sufficient to serve 4 hungry mouths.

MEAT/SAVOURY DISHES TO GO WITH RICE OR NOODLES

(These 'combinations' of dishes are best washed down with a long drink, such as wine or beer or China tea.)

Sliced Beef Quick-fried with Leeks *(for 2-4 people)*

   300-400 g (¾-1 lb) beefsteak
   1 tsp salt
   pepper (to taste)
   2½ tbs vegetable oil
   2 garlic cloves
   4 leeks

1 tbs butter
4-5 tbs chicken stock
2 tsp cornflour (blended in 2 tbs water)
½ tsp sugar
1 tbs soya sauce

Preparation

Cut beef into approximately 4 cm (1½ in) very thin slices. Sprinkle with salt and pepper and rub with ½ tbs oil. Crush and chop garlic, cut leeks slantwise into 2-5 cm (1 in) segments, clean and wash thoroughly.

Cooking

Heat butter and stock in a small saucepan (or wok). When hot add the leeks and turn them over high heat until nearly all the liquid has evaporated (in about 1½-2 mins). Heat remaining oil in a wok. When hot add the beef and garlic. Stir and turn over high heat for 1 min, when the beef should be nearly cooked. Pour in the cornflour mixture, sugar and soya sauce, turn quickly for ½ min with beef when it should give the latter a glossy sheen. Add the leeks into the beef, stir and turn for a further minute. Transfer to a well-heated serving dish. To be served and eaten immediately with rice or noodles.

Quick-fried Beef in Black Bean Sauce with Peppers *(for 2-4 people)*

400 g (1 lb) beefsteak
2 medium green (or red) peppers
3 tsp salted black beans
2½ tbs vegetable oil
½-1 tsp chilli sauce
3 tsp cornflour (blended in 3 tbs water or stock)
1 tbs wine or sherry

Preparation
Cut beef into approximately 4-5 cm (1½-2 in) thin slices.
Remove seeds from the peppers and cut into pieces
approximately the same size as the beef. Soak black beans
in 3 tbs water for 20 mins.

Cooking and Serving
Heat oil in a wok. When hot add beef and turn it quickly in
the hot oil for 1 min and remove with perforated spoon.
Pour the black beans into the wok together with the water
in which they have been soaked. Mix and mash the beans
with the oil against the wok. Add chilli sauce, stir it
once or twice and return the beef into the wok; add the
peppers. Continue to stir and turn them over high heat for
1 min. Add the cornflour mixture evenly into the pan. Stir
and turn the contents and sprinkle with wine or sherry. As
soon as the sauce thickens, transfer the contents onto a
well-heated dish and serve – as with the previous dish – to
be eaten immediately with Fried Rice or Fried Noodles.

Szechuan Hot Chewy Shredded Beef with Carrots and Celery (for 2-4 people)

    400 g (1 lb) beefsteak
    1 tbs soya paste
    ½ tbs soya sauce
    1½ tbs chilli sauce
    1½ tsp sugar
    2½ tbs vegetable oil
    1-2 small dried peppers
    3 sticks celery (shredded)
    ½ tbs lard
    2 medium carrots (shredded)

Preparation
Cut beef into 5 cm (2 in) matchstick (or double matchstick)

size strips. Mix and rub them with soya paste, soya sauce, chilli sauce and sugar. Add ½ tbs oil and continue to mix and rub them together thoroughly. Cut peppers into shreds and remove seeds.

Cooking and Serving
Heat remaining oil in a wok. When hot add beef and stir-fry the shreds over medium heat for 3 mins. Reduce heat to low and continue to stir-fry slowly over low heat for 6-7 mins or until the shredded meat is quite dry and chewy. Add the celery, lard and shredded carrots. Turn the shredded vegetables together with the shredded beef for 2 mins over medium heat. Place the contents in a well-heated serving dish and serve immediately to be eaten with rice and noodles.

Quick-fried Diced Beef with Diced Carrots and Green Peas (for 2-4 people)

  400 g (1 lb) beefsteak
  1 medium carrot
  1-2 slices root-ginger
  4 tbs chicken stock
  1 tbs butter
  1 tbs lard
  100 g (¼ lb) green peas
  2½ tbs vegetable oil
  1 tbs soya sauce
  1 tsp sugar
  ½-¾ tbs soya paste (or hoisin sauce)
  ½ tsp salt
  2 tsp cornflour (blended in 2½ tbs water)

Preparation
Cut beef into small sugar-lump-sized cubes. Dice carrot into similarly sized cubes. Chop and mince root-ginger.

Cooking and Serving

Heat stock in a small pan. Add carrot. Cook over medium heat until the liquid has nearly dried. Add butter and lard and the peas. Leave to cook together for 2 mins and turn them over a few times.

Heat oil in a wok. When hot, add ginger and beef. Stir them quickly over high heat for 1 min. Add soya sauce, sugar, soya paste and salt. Continue to stir and turn quickly for 1 min. Pour in the cornflour mixture. Mix with the beef until it thickens and gives the latter a gloss. Add the carrots and peas into the beef. Stir and mix them together for 30 seconds and serve to be eaten immediately with rice or noodles.

LAMB DISHES

All the foregoing beef dishes can be repeated with lamb which can be prepared, cooked and served in the same manner. In North China where lamb and mutton are very popular, garlic and ginger are invariably added into their cooking and also wine. Where these ingredients are used in the foregoing beef recipes, the quantities of these ingredients can generally be doubled in lamb recipes.

PORK DISHES

There are probably more pork dishes in Chinese cooking than that of any other meat. This is probably because we feel that the taste of pork is more neutral and therefore it is easier to cook and combine with other food materials than any other meat. For instance, the foregoing beef and lamb dishes which are cooked in the wok can all be repeated with pork; except that with pork dishes the sliced, shredded or diced pieces of meat will all have to be stir-fried for 1-2 mins longer than beef or lamb. After the first minute or two of stir-frying, beef hardens with further cooking. Pork does not suffer to the same degree from the same disadvantage; it can stand an extra minute or two of cooking without becoming hard to chew, although it too should not be overcooked, which will make it stiff and dry. It should be cooked to a point where it is still juicy inside but the outside of each piece should, in parts, have become distinctly brown. This is particularly important where there is some fat to the pork, as it is in the browning of the fat that much of the flavour of the pork is derived. Because of the 'neutrality' of pork's savouriness it is often cooked with vegetables which are not extra 'strong' in their flavours (no contrast is required).

Shredded Pork with Spring Onion, Garlic, Pickles and Bean Sprouts *(for 2-3 or more people with other dishes)*

300-400 g (¾-1 lb) lean and fat pork
1 small/medium gherkin
½ tbs cornflour
1 tsp salt
2½ tbs vegetable oil
2 garlic cloves
2 stalks spring onion
300-400 g (¾-1 lb) bean sprouts
1 tbs lard
1½ tbs soya sauce
1 tsp sugar

Preparation

Cut pork and gherkin into slices and then into matchstick shreds. Sprinkle and rub pork with cornflour, salt and ½ tbs oil. Crush and chop garlic. Cut spring onions into 2-5 cm (1 in) long segments.

Cooking

Heat remaining oil in the wok. When hot, add pork and stir-fry over high heat for 2½ mins. Add garlic and spring onions and continue to stir-fry for 1 min. Add bean sprouts and lard, mix, turn and stir-fry them together with the pork until they are evenly mixed. Sprinkle the contents with soya sauce and sugar. Stir-fry for a further 2 mins over high heat and serve.

Serving

Serve to be eaten immediately with rice or noodles.

Stir-fried Sliced Pork with Pepper and Celery *(for 2-3 or more people with other dishes)*

400 g (1 lb) lean and fat pork
1 tsp salt
pepper (to taste)
3 tsp cornflour
2½ tbs vegetable oil
1 red pepper
3 stalks celery
1½ tbs lard or butter
1 tsp sugar
1 tsp chilli sauce
1 tbs soya sauce

Preparation

Cut pork into 4-5 cm (1½-2 in) thin slices. Sprinkle and rub with salt, pepper, cornflour and ½ tbs oil. Cut pepper into 4 cm (1½ in) pieces (remove seeds). Cut celery slantwise into 4 cm (1½ in) segments.

Cooking

Heat remaining oil in a wok. When hot, add the pork and

stir-fry over high heat for 2½ mins. Add pepper, celery, lard, sugar, chilli sauce. Turn and mix them with the pork. Stir-fry them together for 2 mins. Sprinkle contents with soya sauce. Continue to stir-fry for 1 min and serve.

Serving
Serve to be eaten immediately with rice or noodles.

Stir-fried Sliced Pork with Mushrooms and Spring Cabbage (for 2-3 or more people with other dishes)

    400 g (1 lb) lean pork
    ¼ tsp salt
    3 tsp cornflour
    2 tbs vegetable oil
    200 g (½ lb) mushrooms
    300 g (¾ lb) spring cabbage
    2 tbs lard
    1 tbs soya sauce
    3 tbs chicken stock
    ¾ tbs soya paste
    1 tsp sugar

Preparation
Cut pork into 4 cm × 2.5 cm (1½ in × 1 in) thin slices. Sprinkle and rub with salt, cornflour and ½ tbs oil. Remove and discard the stalks of the mushrooms and wash and drain the caps thoroughly. Cut the cabbage into 5 cm (2 in) slices (removing the tougher stalks).

Cooking
Heat lard in a wok. When hot, add the mushrooms and cabbage. Stir-fry over high heat for 1½ mins. Add the soya sauce and stock and continue to stir-fry for 1 min. Place a lid over the wok and leave to cook over medium heat for 2 mins and open the lid.

Heat remaining oil in a second wok. When hot add the pork and stir-fry over high heat for 2½ mins. Add soya paste and sugar and mix and stir with the pork for 2 mins. Add the pork into the first wok containing the vegetables. Stir and mix them together for 1 min and serve.

Serving
Serve to be eaten immediately with rice or noodles.

Shredded Pork with Shredded Bamboo Shoots, Dried Mushrooms, Spring Onions and Transparent Noodles (for 3-4 or more people with other dishes)

300-400 g (¾-1 lb) lean and fat pork
100 g (¼ lb) bamboo shoots
4-5 medium size Chinese dried mushrooms
3 stalks spring onion
50 g (2 oz) transparent pea-starch noodles (will increase in weight 3 times after soaking in water)
2 tbs vegetable oil
1 tbs lard or butter
½ tsp salt
125-250 ml (¼-½ pint) chicken stock
1½ tbs soya sauce
2 tsp sesame oil
2 tbs white wine (or sherry)

Preparation
Cut pork into thin slices and then into matchstick shreds and bamboo shoots into similar shreds. Soak dried mushrooms in water for ½ hour, remove stalks and cut into approximately same size shreds as pork and bamboo shoots. Cut spring onions into 5 cm (2 in) segments. Soak transparent noodles in warm water for 5 mins and drain.

Cooking

Heat oil in a wok. When hot, add pork and stir-fry over high heat for 2 mins. Add lard, mushrooms, bamboo shoots, spring onions and salt. Continue to stir-fry over high heat for 2 mins. Pour in the noodles, chicken stock and soya sauce. Turn the ingredients together until they are well mixed. When contents start to boil, reduce heat and leave to cook slowly for 3 mins. Sprinkle contents with sesame oil and white wine or sherry and serve.

Serving

Serve in a large bowl, to be consumed with rice. This is a dish which is often seen on the table in Chinese homes. It can be re-heated for a second meal if not wholly consumed (unlike the other stir-fried dishes which should be eaten immediately, this dish can be kept for several days in the refrigerator).

Quick-fried Diced Fillet of Pork in Soya Paste Sauce (for 2-4 persons)

    400 g (1 lb) fillet of pork
    ¾ tbs cornflour
    1 egg white
    2½ tbs vegetable oil
    1 tbs lard
    1 tbs soya paste
    2 tsp sugar
    ½ tbs soya sauce
    ½ tbs hoisin sauce (optional)
    1 tbs dry sherry

Preparation

Dice pork into small sugar-lump-sized cubes. Sprinkle and rub with cornflour. Wet with egg white.

Cooking

Heat oil in a wok. When hot, add the cubes of pork and turn them in the hot oil over high heat for 3 mins. Push them to one side of the pan. Add lard to the other side. When it has melted add soya paste, sugar, soya sauce, hoisin sauce (if used) and sherry. Mix them together over medium heat into a thickened boiling sauce. Bring over the pork cubes to mix with the sauce. Stir and turn for 1 min over high heat and serve.

Serving

To be served and eaten immediately with a copious amount of fried rice or plain boiled rice, as this dish is quite salty.

'Trilogy of Pork' Quick-fried with Soya Paste and Diced Cucumbers *(for 2-3 people or more with other dishes)*

140-200 g (⅓-½ lb) fillet of pork
140 g (⅓ lb) pork liver
140 g (⅓ lb) pork kidney
2½ tbs vegetable oil
2 slices root-ginger (chopped and minced)
7.5 cm (3 in) section of medium cucumber
1 tbs lard
1 tbs soya paste
½ tbs soya sauce
1½ tsp sugar
1 tbs dry sherry

Preparation

Dice pork, liver and kidney into 6 mm (¼ in) cubes (after removing membrane, gristle etc.). Rub them with ½ tbs oil and minced root-ginger. Cut cucumber (including skin) into similarly sized cubes.

Cooking

Heat remaining oil in a wok. When hot, add the meat cubes and stir-fry them over high heat for 3½ mins and push them to one side of the wok. Add lard to the other side and when it has melted add soya paste, soya sauce, sugar and sherry and mix them all into a thickened boiling sauce. Bring the cubed meats over to mix with the sauce. Stir-fry them together for 30 seconds. Add cucumber cubes and stir-fry them together for a further 30 seconds and serve.

Serving

Serve to be eaten immediately with plain boiled rice or fried rice.

CHICKEN DISHES

To us Chinese chicken meat has one similarity to pork which is that its flavour is 'neutral' which makes it easy to combine and cook with other ingredients to produce a wide variety of dishes. There are, therefore, nearly as many chicken dishes in Chinese cooking as there are pork dishes. The principal difference being that chicken, unlike pork, does not occur in large pieces or slices, and is therefore often chopped through the bones or cooked with the bones. In instances where chicken is cooked without bones (breast of chicken, or pieces where bones are removed), it is treated almost precisely like pork, except that it requires somewhat shorter cooking – in stir-frying in the wok over high heat, this means simply shortening the cooking by a minute to 1½ mins. When cooking in somewhat larger pieces, chicken is usually cooked chopped through the bones into large bite-size pieces. To cook these in the wok, they would usually require 3-4 mins braising in addition to the initial stir-frying. In the first three of the following recipes we have the breast of chicken meat cooked and treated in the same manner as pork would be treated.

'Trilogy of Chicken' Quick-fried with Small Button Mushrooms and Green Peas (for 3-4 people or more with other dishes)

    140-200 g (⅓-½ lb) breast of chicken
    50-75 g (2-3 oz) chicken liver
    50-75 g (2-3 oz) chicken kidney
    ½ tsp salt
    2 slices root-ginger (minced)
    2½ tbs vegetable oil
    1 tbs lard or butter
    75-100 g (3-4 oz) small button mushrooms (often sold in cans)
    75-100 g (3-4 oz) peas (frozen)
    1 tbs soya sauce
    ½ tsp sugar
    1½ tbs dry sherry

Preparation

Cut or dice chicken meat, liver and kidney into small sugar-lump-sized pieces. Rub them with salt and minced ginger and ½ tbs oil. Leave to season for 15 mins.

Cooking

Heat remaining oil in the wok. When hot add all the chicken meat, liver and kidney. Stir-fry them over high heat for 2 mins. Push them to one side, add lard and, when melted, add mushrooms and peas. Stir them in the hot fat, sprinkle the contents with soya sauce, sugar and sherry. Turn, mix and stir-fry all the ingredients together over high heat for 1½ mins.

Serving

The dish should be served and eaten immediately with fried rice or plain boiled rice.

Diced Chicken Quick-fried with Cashew Nuts in Soya Paste Sauce *(for 2-3 or more people with other dishes) dishes)*

200 g (½ lb) chicken breast
2 slices root-ginger
2 tbs vegetable oil
200 g (½ lb) cashew nuts
1 tbs lard
1 tbs soya paste
1½ tsp sugar
½ tbs soya sauce
1 tbs dry sherry
1½ tbs chicken stock

Preparation
Dice chicken into small sugar-lump-sized cubes. Mince ginger and rub it on the chicken.

Cooking
Heat oil in a wok. Add chicken and cashew nuts and stir-fry them over high heat for 2½ mins. Remove with perforated spoon. Add lard. When it has melted, add soya paste, sugar, soya sauce, sherry and stock. Stir and mix them over high heat into a thickened boiling sauce. Return the chicken and nuts into the wok. Turn and stir-fry the chicken and nuts in the sauce for 1 min and serve.

Serving
Serve to be eaten immediately with fried rice or plain boiled rice.

Quick-fried Shredded Chicken with French Beans *(for 3-4 people or more with other dishes)*

200-300 g (½-¾ lb) French beans

140-200 g (⅓-½ lb) breast of chicken
½ tsp salt
pepper (to taste)
¾ tbs cornflour
1 egg white
¼ chicken stock cube
5-6 tbs chicken stock
½ tbs soya sauce
1 tbs sherry
1 tbs lard
2 tbs vegetable oil

Preparation
Top and tail the beans. Cut breast of chicken into double
matchstick shreds. Sprinkle and rub with salt, pepper and
cornflour and wet with egg white. Dissolve stock cube in
stock.

Cooking
Heat stock, soya sauce and sherry in a flat-bottomed pan
(saucepan or frying-pan). When the liquid starts to boil
add the beans and spread them out in a single layer.
Reduce heat and leave them to cook for about 4-5 mins or
until nearly all the liquid has evaporated. Add the lard and
turn the beans in the melted fat until they are evenly
covered. Reduce heat to very low and leave the beans to
cook at a low simmer. Meanwhile, heat oil over medium
heat in a wok. Swill it so that the bottom of the wok is
evenly covered. Pour in the shredded chicken. Spread it
out in a single layer, turn and stir-fry gently for 1½ mins.
Add the beans from the pan into the wok. Turn and toss to
mix them with the shredded chicken for 1 min when the
contents should be ready to serve.

Serving
Serve to be eaten immediately with plain boiled rice or

fried rice. The contrast between the greenness of the beans and the pure whiteness of the chicken and their contrast in texture make this a very appealing dish.

Kung-Po 'Hot Fried' Chicken Cubes with Peppers (for 2-3 or more people)

    200-250 g (8-10 oz) breast of chicken
    1 tsp salt
    2 tsp cornflour
    2 tbs vegetable oil
    1 green sweet pepper
    2 dried chilli peppers
    1 tbs lard

For Sauce
    3 tbs stock
    1½ tbs vinegar
    1 tbs tomato puree
    1 tbs dry sherry
    1½ tsp sherry
    2 tsp cornflour

Preparation
Dice chicken into small sugar-lump-sized cubes. Sprinkle with salt and cornflour and rub with ½ tbs oil. Cut sweet pepper into 2.5 cm (1 in) pieces (remove seeds). Chop dried chilli pepper (removing seeds) into fine shreds. Mix sauce ingredients into consistent mixture.

Cooking
Heat remaining oil in a wok. When hot add the chicken cubes and stir-fry over high heat for 2 mins and remove with perforated spoon. Add lard. When it has melted add dried peppers. Stir them a few times over high heat, add the sweet peppers and sauce mixture. Stir until the sauce

starts to boil. Return the chicken into the pan. Turn and stir the chicken with the other ingredients for 1½ mins and serve.

Serving

Serve to be eaten immediately with plain boiled rice or fried rice. This is a well-known Szechuan dish which appeals to those who like their food hot and spicy.

Stir-fried Shredded Chicken with Shredded Ham, Mushrooms, Celery and Transparent Noodles *(for 3-4 or 5 people)*

   200 g (8 oz) breast of chicken
   ½ tsp salt
   100-125 g (4-5 oz) ham
   2-3 sticks of celery
   4 large Chinese dried mushrooms
   50-75 g (2-3 oz) transparent pea-starch noodles (should
      increase weight by 3 times when soaked)
   2-3 stalks spring onion
   2 tbs vegetable oil
   1 tbs lard
   250 ml (½ pint) chicken stock
   ½ chicken stock cube
   1 tbs soya sauce
   2 tsp sesame oil

Preparation

Cut chicken into double matchstick shreds and rub with salt. Cut ham and celery into similarly sized shreds. Soak mushrooms in water for 30 mins and cut into similar shreds as the ham, after removing stalks. Soak noodles in water 4-5 mins and drain. Cut spring onions into 4 cm (1½ in) segments.

Cooking

Heat oil in a wok. When hot, add the chicken and stir-fry over high heat for 1½ mins and remove with perforated spoon. Add the lard and mushrooms. After stir-frying for 1 min, add ham and celery. Turn and stir-fry them together for 2 mins. Pour in the stock and add the noodles, sprinkle with crumbled stock cube and spring onion segments. Return the shredded chicken, turn and mix them with the other ingredients in the wok. When contents start to boil, reduce heat to low, sprinkle them with soya sauce and leave them to cook together for 4-5 mins. Sprinkle with sesame oil and serve.

Serving

Serve in a large bowl. As this is quite a bulky dish, it can go a long way if eaten with plain boiled rice or fried rice.

In the following three dishes, chicken is cooked on the bone – by chopping the chicken through the bones into 16 to 20 pieces. The stir-frying here is followed by a short period of braising.

Quick-fried Chicken Braised in Black Bean Sauce (for 5-6 or more people with other dishes)

   1 medium-sized chicken (1-1.5 kg or 2½-3½ lb)
   1 tsp salt
   pepper (to taste)
   3 slices root-ginger
   5-6 tbs vegetable oil
   1½ tbs black beans
   2 medium onions
   1 green or red sweet pepper
   1½ tbs lard
   4 tbs good stock
   2 tbs wine or sherry

Preparation

Chop chicken through the bone into 20 pieces (remove and discard head and innards). Sprinkle and rub with salt, pepper and chopped ginger and finally with 1 tbs oil. Soak black beans in 4 tbs water for 15 mins and drain. Cut onions into thin slices and sweet pepper into 2.5 cm × 4 cm (1 in × 1½ in) pieces (remove seeds).

Cooking

Heat remaining oil in a wok. When hot, add the chicken pieces and stir-fry over high heat for 5 mins. Remove chicken with perforated spoon and pour away any excess oil. Add lard and onion into the wok. Stir them together over high heat for 1 min. Add the black beans, mash them in the oil against the wok and onion. Pour in the stock, wine or sherry and add the peppers. Stir them together until contents are boiling. Return the chicken pieces into the wok and turn and stir them with the other ingredients. Leave them to cook for 3-4 mins. Turn them once more and serve.

Serving

Serve in a large bowl or deep-sided dish to be eaten immediately with plain boiled rice or fried rice. The detaching of the meat from the bone in the mouth, which the Chinese are adept at, requires practice on the part of westerners.

Hung Shao Chicken or 'People's Coq au Vin' *(for 5-8 people with other dishes)*

3 slices root-ginger
1 medium-sized chicken (1-5kg or 2½-3½ lb)
5-6 tbs vegetable oil
125 ml (¼ pint) water
125 ml (¼ pint) red or white wine

5 tbs soya sauce
2 tsp sugar

Preparation
Shred the ginger. Chop chicken through bone into about
20 pieces. Rub with ginger and 1 tbs oil.

Cooking
Heat remaining oil in the wok. When hot add the chicken
and stir-fry over high heat for 5-6 mins. Pour away any
excess oil and add water, wine, soya sauce and sugar. Stir
and mix them well with the chicken. When the liquid starts
to boil, turn the chicken in the sauce for 2-3 mins. Reduce
heat to a simmer and leave the contents to cook gently
under cover for 25 mins.

Serving
Serve in a large bowl or deep-sided dish, to be eaten with
plain boiled rice or fried rice. The dish can be kept for 2-3
days in the refrigerator and re-heated when required.

Quick-fried and Braised Chicken in Curry Sauce *(for 5-8 people with other dishes)*

1 medium-sized chicken (1-1.5 kg or 2½-3½ lb)
3 slices root-ginger
2 tsp salt
5-6 tbs vegetable oil
2 medium onions
3 garlic cloves
1½ tbs lard
1½-2 tbs curry powder
5-6 tbs stock
1 tbs soya sauce

Preparation

Chop chicken through bone into 20 pieces. Shred and mince ginger. Sprinkle and rub chicken with salt, ginger and 1 tbs oil. Cut onions into thin slices. Crush and chop garlic.

Cooking

Heat remaining oil in the wok. When hot, add the chicken pieces. Turn and stir-fry over high heat for 5-6 mins. Remove chicken with perforated spoon and pour away any excess oil. Add lard into the wok. When it has melted, add onion, garlic and curry powder. Stir-fry in the hot fat for 2 mins over high heat. Pour in the stock and soya sauce. Mix them well with the other ingredients. When the stock starts to boil vigorously, return the chicken into the wok. Mix the chicken with the sauce and other ingredients. Reduce heat to low and leave contents to cook for 5-6 mins.

Serving

Serve in a large bowl or deep-sided dish, to be eaten with plain boiled rice or fried rice.

Quick-fried and Braised Lemon Chicken *(for 3-5 or more people with other dishes)*

> ½ medium chicken (1-1.5 kg or 2½-3½ lb)
> 1 tsp salt
> cornflour
> 2 slices root-ginger
> 1 egg white
> 3-4 Chinese dried mushrooms
> 1 red sweet pepper
> peel of 2 lemons
> 3 stalks spring onion
> 1 large lemon
> 5-6 tbs vegetable oil

1½ tbs lard
3 tbs chicken stock
1 tbs dry sherry
1 tbs soya sauce
2 tsp sugar

Preparation

Bone the chicken. Cut meat into 4 cm (1½ in) slices or strips. Sprinkle with salt, cornflour and chopped ginger and wet with egg white. Soak dried mushrooms in water for 30 mins. Remove stalks and cut into large matchstick shreds. Cut pepper (after removing seeds) and lemon peel into similar thin shreds (only the outer skin). Cut spring onions into 6 cm (2½ in) segments. Squeeze the juice from lemon.

Cooking

Heat oil in a wok. When hot, add the chicken and stir-fry quickly over high heat for 3 mins and remove with perforated spoon. Pour away excess oil. Add lard. When it has melted add mushrooms, pepper and spring onion. Stir them in the hot fat over high heat for 1 min. Add stock, sherry, soya sauce and sugar. When the contents start to boil return the chicken pieces into the wok. After stirring them around for 1 min sprinkle contents with lemon peel and lemon juice. Turn them around with the other ingredients for 1 min and serve.

Serving

Serve on a well-heated dish to be eaten immediately with plain boiled rice or fried rice.

VEGETABLE DISHES

In a Chinese meal, there is usually a pure vegetable dish in spite of the fact that many of the dishes on the table are already mixed dishes of vegetable and meat. But pure vegetable dishes are imperative if some dishes on the table are of pure meat.

Chinese vegetables are either quick-fried or shortly braised. Both methods of cooking can be very conveniently carried out in the wok.

Quick Stir-fried Spinach *(for 2-3 or 4 people with other dishes)*

    400 g (1 lb) spinach
    2 garlic cloves
    2 slices root-ginger
    3 tbs vegetable oil
    1½ tbs soya sauce
    1½ tbs chicken stock
    1½ tbs lard

Preparation
Remove the tougher stems and discoloured leaves of the spinach and cut or tear leaves into 7.5-10 cm (3-4 in) pieces. Crush and chop garlic, shred and mince ginger.

Cooking
Heat oil in the wok. When hot, add the garlic and ginger. Turn them around once in the hot oil. Add spinach. Turn and stir and mix them with the oil and the other ingredients over high heat for 1½ mins. Reduce heat and sprinkle contents with soya sauce and stock. Mix them evenly with the vegetables. Stir quickly until ⅔ of the liquid has evaporated. Add the lard. Stir and mix it with the vegetable. This should enrich it and give it a gloss.

Serving
Serve to be eaten immediately with boiled or fried rice and other dishes.

Quick Stir-fried Spring Greens (or Cabbage) (for 2-3 or 4 people)

Spring greens can be cooked in precisely the same manner as spinach (see the previous recipe), except that the leaves of 'greens' can be slightly thicker and tougher and therefore require a minute and a half's extra cooking. This is done by adding 3 tbs of chicken stock instead of 1½ and stir-frying at this stage is prolonged by 1½ mins before the lard is added for the final 'glossing' and stir-frying together.

Quick-fried Leeks (for 2-3 or 4 people)

Leeks, like spring greens, can be cooked in exactly the same manner as spinach, except that, like spring onions, leeks are more often than not, in the Chinese tradition, cooked in this manner with a small amount of meat (ie pork, lamb or beef). For 400 g (1 lb) of leeks (which need to be thoroughly washed and rinsed) about 100 g (¼ lb) of meat can be cooked with it. The meat should be cut into small and very thin slices and rubbed with a small amount of salt, cornflour and wetted with egg white. It should be stir-fried for 1½ mins with ginger and garlic before the leeks are added. Whereupon the ingredients should be stir-fried for 1½ mins together before the soya sauce and stock are added. When the liquid has half evaporated, lard is added for the final 'glossing' and stir-frying together for ½ min before serving.

TWO-VEGETABLE DISHES

A different type of vegetable is often added to the spinach, spring greens or leeks to produce a 'mixed vegetable' dish. In these cases, the second vegetable (such as mushrooms or

Chinese dried mushrooms, aubergines or courgettes) is treated in the same manner as meat in the previous recipe – it is sliced thinly, cooked or stir-fried first with garlic and ginger before the spinach, greens or leeks are added. Because of the added quantity of vegetables being stir-fried, an additional ½-1 tbs of oil may be used for the initial stir-frying.

Quick-fried and Braised Vegetable Dishes

Quick-fried and Braised Celery (for 3-4 people or more with other dishes)

4-6 stalks of celery (about 400 g or 1 lb)
2 slices root-ginger
2½ tbs vegetable oil
1½ tbs soya sauce
1 tbs hoisin sauce
4 tbs chicken stock
½ chicken stock cube
1 tbs lard or butter

Preparation
Clean celery thoroughly, and cut slantwise into 5 cm (2 in) segments. Shred ginger.

Cooking
Heat oil in a wok. When hot, add ginger. Stir it around in the hot oil for ½ min. Add celery and stir-fry over high heat for 1½ mins. Pour in soya sauce, hoisin sauce and chicken stock. Sprinkle contents with crumbled stock cube. Stir-fry them all together for 2 mins. Reduce heat and place a lid over the wok and leave to simmer for 4 mins. Add lard, and turn contents over a few more times and serve.

Serving
Serve in a bowl or deep-sided dish to be eaten with boiled or fried rice.

Quick-fried and Braised Broccoli *(for 3-4 people or more with other dishes)*

Break brocolli (about 400 g or 1 lb) into individual flowerets and cook them in exactly the same manner and for the same length of time as celery (see the above recipe). Serve with boiled or fried rice.

Quick-fried and Braised Cauliflower *(for 3-4 people or more with other dishes)*

Cook and treat the cauliflower in the same manner using the same ingredients as broccoli in the previous recipe. In the Chinese tradition, the cauliflower is often sprinkled with one or two tablespoons of minced ham when served.

Quick-fried and Braised French Beans *(for 3-4 people or more with other dishes)*

   400 g (1 lb) French beans
   2 tbs vegetable oil
   4-5 tbs chicken stock

For Sauce
   2 slices ginger
   1 tbs lard
   3-4 tbs minced pork
   1 tbs soya sauce
   1½ tsp bean curd cheese (often called bean curd sauce or paste in Chinese food stores)
   1 tbs hoisin sauce
   1 tbs sherry
   1 tsp sugar

Preparation

Clean and top and tail the beans. Chop and mince ginger.

Cooking

Heat oil in the wok. Add beans and stir-fry them over medium heat for 2 mins. Add chicken stock and stir-fry them again for 1 min. Reduce heat and leave them to simmer for 4-5 mins, when nearly all the liquid will have evaporated. Remove the beans with a perforated spoon and put aside. Add lard into the wok. When it has melted add minced meat and minced ginger. Stir them over high heat for 1½ mins. Add the soya sauce, bean curd cheese, hoisin sauce, sugar and sherry. Stir and mix them together with the ginger and minced meat. As the sauce starts to bubble and thicken, return the beans into the wok. Stir and turn them quickly in the sauce until every bean is well covered. Dish out and serve.

Serving

Serve on a well-heated dish to be consumed with plain boiled rice or fried rice.

'Red-Cooked' Chinese Cabbage *(for 4-5 or more people with other dishes)*

'Red-cooking' is simply the process of cooking or braising with soya sauce and is used extensively for cooking both meat and vegetables.

   1 large Chinese (or Savoy) cabbage (about 1-1.5 kg or
     2½-3½ lb)
   2 tbs vegetable oil
   1½ tbs lard
   2½ tbs soya sauce
   4-5 tbs chicken stock (or bone stock)
   2 tsp sugar
   ½ chicken stock cube

Preparation

Clean cabbage and cut into 5 cm (2 in) slices.

Cooking

Heat oil and lard at the bottom of the wok. When hot add
the cabbage and turn it slowly in the fat over high heat for
3 mins until each leaf is well covered. Sprinkle the soya
sauce, stock, sugar and crumbled stock cube. Continue to
stir and turn until all the ingredients are well mixed.
Reduce heat to low and leave contents to cook gently for
10 mins.

Serving

Serve in a large bowl or deep-sided dish. This dish is
excellent with plain rice, fried rice or noodles.

'White-Cooked' Cabbage *(for 4-5 or more people with other dishes)*

1 large Chinese (or Savoy) cabbage (about 1-1.5 kg or
  2½-3 lb)
2 tbs vegetable oil
1½ tbs lard
1½ tbs dried shrimps
250 ml (½ pint) good stock (chicken or bone)
1 chicken stock cube
1 tsp salt
pepper (to taste)
1½ tsp sesame oil

Preparation

Clean cabbage and cut into 5 cm (2 in) slices. Shred the
ginger.

Cooking

Heat oil and lard in the wok. When hot, add ginger and

shrimps. Turn them a couple of times in the hot fat. Add the cabbage. Turn and stir them with the other ingredients over high heat for 2 mins. Pour in the stock, sprinkle the contents with crumbled stock cube, salt and pepper (to taste). When contents start to boil, reduce heat to low, and leave to cook gently under cover for 10 mins. Turn contents over once or twice, sprinkle with sesame oil and serve.

Serving
Serve in a large bowl or deep-sided dish. This dish is excellent with rice or noodles.

THE AUGMENTATION OF MEAT THROUGH VEGETABLES

Quick-fried and braised mixed vegetable dishes with minced meat (meat is used here mainly for flavouring and only in small quantities).

Quick-fried and Braised Marrow with Minced Pork (for 3-4 or more people with other dishes)

400 g (1 lb) marrow (a cut from a large marrow)
½ tsp salt
pepper (to taste)
½ chicken stock cube
250 ml (½ pint) good stock
2 garlic cloves
2½ tbs vegetable oil
1½ tbs lard
100 g (¼ lb) minced pork
1¼ tbs soya sauce
½ tbs hoisin sauce (optional)
½ tsp sugar
1½ tbs dry sherry

Preparation
Peel away the skin of the marrow. Cut marrow into 7.5 cm
× 4 cm (3 in × 1½ in) pieces. Sprinkle them evenly with
salt and pepper. Dissolve stock cube in hot stock. Crush
and chop garlic.

Cooking
Heat oil in the wok. Add marrow pieces and turn them in
the oil over medium heat for 1½-2 mins until each piece of
marrow is well covered with hot oil. Pour the stock evenly
over the marrow. Turn the marrow in the stock for a
minute. When contents start to boil, reduce heat and leave
them to simmer gently for 4-5 mins. Pour the marrow and
liquid into a basin and leave aside. Heat lard in the wok.
Add minced pork and garlic. Stir and turn them over high
heat for 1 min. Add soya sauce, hoisin sauce (if used),
sugar and sherry. Continue to stir-fry them together for 2-3
mins. Return the marrow to the wok. Spoon some minced
meat over each piece of marrow. When contents start to
boil, reduce heat to a simmer and leave them to cook
gently for 4-5 mins.

Serving
Serve in a large bowl or deep-sided dish. An excellent and
inexpensive dish to serve with rice or noodles.

**Quick-fried and Braised Aubergines and Courgettes with
Minced Beef** *(for 3-5 or more people with one or two
other dishes)*

   200-300 g (½-¾ lb) courgettes
   200-300 g (½-¾ lb) aubergines
   salt and pepper (to taste)
   2½ tbs vegetable oil
   2 slices root-ginger
   ½ chicken stock cube

250 ml (½ pint) good stock
1½ tbs lard
100 g (¼ lb) minced beef
1¼ tbs soya sauce
½ tbs hoisin sauce (optional)
1 tbs dry sherry
½ tsp sugar

Preparation
Cut courgettes into 12 mm (½ in) thick slices. Cut aubergines into slices of similar thickness. Sprinkle and rub with salt and pepper and ½ tbs oil. Shred and mince ginger. Dissolve stock cube in hot stock.

Cooking
Heat remaining oil in the wok. When hot, add courgettes and aubergines. Turn them in the oil over high heat for 1½ mins. Pour in the stock. Turn the vegetables in the stock. When contents start to boil, reduce heat and leave contents to simmer gently for 5-6 mins. Remove from wok, put in a basin and leave aside. Heat lard in the wok. When hot, add the minced beef and ginger. Stir them over high heat for 2 mins. Pour in the soya sauce, hoisin sauce (if used), sherry and sugar. Stir them together still over high heat for 2 more mins. Add the aubergines and courgettes into the wok. Mix them gently with the beef and leave contents to simmer gently for a further 4-5 mins.

Serving
Serve in a bowl or deep-sided dish to be eaten with rice or noodles.

Quick-fried and Braised Bean Curd and Chinese Dried Mushrooms with Minced Pork (or Beef) (for 3-4 or more people with one or two other dishes)

2-3 cakes bean curd

6-8 medium/large Chinese dried mushrooms
2 stalks spring onion
½ chicken stock cube
125 ml (¼ pint) good stock
2½ tbs vegetable oil
1½ tbs lard
100 g (¼ lb) minced pork (or beef)
1½ tbs soya sauce
½ tbs soya paste (or hoisin sauce)
1 tsp sugar
½ tsp chilli sauce
1 tbs dry sherry

Preparation
Cut each cake of bean curd into about a dozen pieces.
Soak mushrooms in water for 30 mins, remove stalks and
cut each cap into 4 pieces. Cut spring onions into 2.5 cm (1
in) sections. Dissolve stock cube in hot stock.

Cooking
Heat oil in the wok. Add bean curd pieces, turn them in the
hot oil for 1½ mins. Pour in the stock. Turn the bean curd
in the stock for 1 min. Leave contents to simmer for 3-4
mins. Remove and put aside. Heat lard in the wok. When
it has melted, add minced meat and mushrooms. Stir-fry
them over high heat for 3 mins. Add soya sauce, soya
paste, sugar, chilli sauce, spring onion and sherry. Stir
them all together over high heat for 2 mins. Return the
bean curd and stock into the wok. Turn the minced beef
and sauce gently over the bean curd. Leave to simmer over
low heat for 4-5 mins.

Serving
Serve in a large bowl or deep-sided dish to be eaten with
plain boiled rice or fried rice.

Quick-fried and Braised Bean Curd with Minced Meat in a Hot Sauce *(for 3-4 or more people with one or two other dishes)*

2 cakes bean curd
4 large Chinese dried mushrooms
3 garlic cloves
2 dried chilli peppers
2 stalks spring onion
½ chicken stock cube
250 ml (½ pint) good stock
2 tbs lard
200 g (½ lb) minced pork
1½ tbs soya sauce
1½ tsp sugar
1 tbs soya paste (or hoisin sauce)
4-5 tbs green peas
3 tsp cornflour (blended in 3 tbs water or stock)
2 tbs dry sherry

Preparation
Cut bean curd into small sugar-lump-sized pieces. Soak mushrooms in water for 30 mins, remove stalks and chop caps into small pieces (or mince coarsely). Crush and chop garlic. Cut peppers, remove seeds and chop into small fine pieces. Mince spring onions coarsely. Dissolve stock cube in hot stock.

Cooking
Heat bean curd in stock in a saucepan. When contents start to boil leave to simmer for 3-4 mins. Heat lard in a wok. When hot, add minced meat, garlic and chilli peppers. Stir-fry them over high heat for 3-4 mins. Add soya sauce, sugar, soya paste and spring onion. Continue to stir-fry for 2 mins. Add the bean curd. Mash them with the other ingredients against the sides of the wok. Stir and mix them

all together. Add the green peas and leave the contents to simmer gently together for 4-5 mins. Sprinkle the blended cornflour evenly over the contents. Turn and stir until the sauce thickens. Sprinkle with sherry.

Serving
Serve in a bowl, or deep-sided dish. To be eaten with plain boiled rice or fried rice. Bean curd so cooked is peculiar to the province of Szechuan and is much loved by people who like spicy foods.

Soups

Chinese soup dishes are frequently, although not invariably, a blend of meat and vegetables in a meat-based broth or stock. Although the stock may have taken a good length of time to prepare, through long simmering together of bone and meat (ie carcass of duck or chicken or head and tail of fish), the final blending together of meat and vegetable is usually a very quick affair done in a wok, almost in an instant. The soup plays an important part in a Chinese meal, as we do not drink water at meal times and wine only very infrequently and usually only at banquets. Soup also has a different function in a Chinese meal compared to a western meal; in a Chinese meal, it is meant to be a lubricant to wash down mouthfuls of bulk and savoury foods. Therefore, it is usually a clear soup, or a *consommé* in which some pieces of thinly-sliced meat and leaves of vegetables are floating and immersed to provide variation in colour and substance, as well as textural contrast. It is seldom a thick soup, unlike most western soups, which are often used to provide additional bulk to the meal. Because Chinese soups are usually clear, making them presents an opportunity to blend flavours in purely liquid form (like making a cocktail). The addition of fresh meat and vegetables during the final 'blending' together provides the further opportunity of adding freshness to the savoury concoction as well as the final opportunity of providing colour and texture to the product. It is not unlike the making of a punch in the western sense (albeit a hot and savoury 'punch'!). The aim is to produce high savouriness in a clear liquid form with the added introduction of the quality of freshness and the appeal of colour and textural interest in the last blending together of a selection of different food materials and ingredients.

The Basic Stock for Soups

In the following recipes it is presumed that the 'basic stock' required for the making of soups is already available in the kitchen. This can be readily made by simmering a carcass of chicken or duck with a piece or two of meaty bone in 1.5-2 litres (3-4 pints) of water for 2-3 hours. Into the pot should be added 2-3 slices of root-ginger, which can reduce rankness or rawness (or chemical taste in the flavour of battery-raised poultry). Seasonings should be added, including one chicken stock cube just before filtering and dishing out the stock for use.

'Soup of the Gods' (for 4-5 people)

This is one of the simplest of all soups, which is usually prepared in the Chinese home for visitors who arrive for dinner unannounced.

  1 egg
  2 stalks spring onion
  750 ml-1 litre (1½-2 pints) basic stock
  salt and pepper (to taste)
  ½-1 tsp sesame oil

Preparation

Beat egg in a bowl or cup with a fork for 10-12 seconds. Cut or chop spring onions (including all green parts) into coarse mince or shavings.

Cooking

Heat stock in the wok. When it starts to boil, reduce heat

to a simmer. Add salt and pepper to taste. Pour in the beaten egg in very thin stream, along the prongs of a fork evenly over the surface of the stock. Pour the stock into a large soup bowl or tureen. Sprinkle the chopped spring onions and sesame oil over the surface of the soup.

Serving
Serve at the centre of the table for the diners to help themselves, or the soup can be divided into individual dishes and served in the conventional western manner; but it must be borne in mind that Chinese soups are meant to be drunk not just at the beginning of the meal but in mouthfuls throughout the meal.

Spinach and Bean Curd Soup *(for 4-6 people)*

This is another of those homely soups which is often seen on Chinese family dinner-tables.

    200 g (½ lb) spinach (or young spring greens)
    1 cake bean curd (optional)
    2 tbs vegetable oil
    750 ml-1 litre (1½-2 pints) basic stock
    1 chicken stock cube
    salt and pepper to taste)
    1 tsp sesame oil

Preparation
Remove the tougher stalks of the spinach and cut or tear into 7.5-10 cm (3-4 in) pieces. Cut bean curd into approximately 20 similarly sized pieces.

Cooking and Serving
Heat oil in the wok. When hot, turn the vegetable in it over medium heat for 2 mins intil it is well lubricated. Pour in the stock, add stock cube and bean curd. Bring to boil and

simmer gently for 4-5 mins. Sprinkle with salt and pepper
and sesame oil. Serve as in the previous recipe.

'Green Jade' Soup *(for 4-6 people)*

 100 g (¼ lb) frozen minced spinach (or mince 100 g (¼
  (¼ lb) fresh spinach finely in a blender)
 50-75 g (2-3 oz) breast of chicken
 1 tbs lard
 750 ml-1 litre (1½-2 pints) basic stock
 1 chicken stock cube
 1 tbs soya sauce
 salt and pepper to taste
 1½ tbs cornflour (blended in 4 tbs water)

Preparation
Thaw the spinach if frozen. Chop chicken into fine mince.

Cooking and Serving
Heat lard in the wok. Add spinach and chicken. Turn them
over medium heat for 2½ mins. Pour in the stock, add
stock cube and soya sauce. Bring contents to a gentle boil.
Simmer for 3-4 mins. Adjust for seasoning with salt and
pepper. Add cornflour mixture. Stir until the soup has
slightly thickened. Serve as in the previous recipe.

Chicken and Mushroom Soup *(for 4-6 people)*

This is a popular soup which is as easy to make as others.
The mushroom flavour is enhanced if some Chinese dried
mushrooms are used in addition to ordinary mushrooms.

 100 g (¼ lb) breast of chicken (or lean pork)
 ½ tsp salt
 ½ tbs cornflour
 ½ egg white

100 g (¼ lb) button mushrooms
4-6 medium size Chinese dried mushrooms (optional)
1½ tbs lard
875 ml-1 litre (1¾-2 pints) good stock
1 tbs soya sauce
1 chicken stock cube
salt and pepper (to taste)

Preparation

Cut chicken (or pork) into 2.5 cm × 18 mm (1 in × ¾ in) thin slices. Rub with salt and cornflour, and wet with egg white. Wash mushrooms thoroughly and cut into thin slices (including stalks). If Chinese dried mushrooms are used, soak them in warm water for 25-30 mins, remove and discard stalks and cut caps into quarters.

Cooking and Serving

Heat lard in the wok. When hot, add chicken and dried mushrooms. Turn them gently in the hot fat for 1½ mins. Pour in the stock and add the fresh mushrooms. Bring contents to boil, reduce heat to low and simmer gently for 5-6 mins. Add soya sauce and stock cube and adjust seasoning with salt and pepper. Stir a few times and serve the soup as in the previous recipes.

Crab-Meat, Chicken and Sweet Corn Soup *(for 4-6 people)*

This is a very popular soup in Chinese restaurants in the west.

75-100 g (3-4 oz) breast of chicken
75-100 g (3-4 oz) crab-meat (fresh or canned)
2 stalks spring onion
1½ tbs lard
375 ml (¾ pint) good stock
200 g (8 oz) sweet corn

1 chicken stock cube
salt and pepper (to taste)
1½ tbs cornflour (blended in 5 tbs water)

Preparation

Shred the chicken. Flake the crab meat. Cut spring onion into fine shavings.

Cooking and Serving

Heat lard in the wok. When hot, add spring onion and chicken. Stir them in the hot fat for 1 min. Add the crabmeat and stir them together for another minute. Pour in the stock and add the sweet corn. Bring to boil, reduce heat to low, simmer and cook gently for 7-8 mins, stirring occasionally. Add stock cube and adjust seasoning with salt and pepper. Stir and pour in the cornflour mixture. Stir until the soup thickens. Serve as in the previous recipes – in a large soup bowl for the diners to help themselves throughout the meal or serve in individual bowls in the conventional manner.

Hot and Sour Soup *(for 4-6 people)*

A popular North China soup, which is also called 'junk soup' as almost anything can be thrown in to make up the bulk of the soup, which is finished off with the addition of the 'hot and sour sauce' which gives it its characteristic impact.

4-6 medium-sized Chinese dried mushrooms
2-3 tbs 'wood ears' (optional)
25-50 g (1-2 oz) ham
1 or 2 cakes bean curd
1½ tbs lard
75-100 g (3-4 oz) lean and fat pork (cooked or fresh)
2-3 tbs shrimps or prawns

875 ml (1¾ pints) stock
1 chicken stock cube
2-3 tsp dried shrimps

Sauce

2 tbs cornflour (blended in 6 tbs water)
1½ tbs soya sauce
4-6 tbs vinegar
¼-½ tsp freshly-ground black pepper

Preparation

Soak dried mushrooms in warm water for 30 mins. Discard stalks, and cut each cap into 6-8 pieces (retain mushroom water). Soak 'wood ears' in water for 30 mins. Rinse and drain. Cut ham into small pieces. Mix the sauce ingredients into a sauce. Cut each bean curd into 4-6 mm (1/6-¼ in) cubes.

Cooking and Serving

Heat lard in the wok. Add pork, mushrooms and dried shrimps. Stir them together over medium heat for 1½ mins. Add stock, stock cube, fresh shrimps, 'wood ears', ham and mushroom water. Bring to boil, reduce heat to a simmer and cook gently for 10 mins. Add the sauce and stir until soup thickens. Serve as in previous recipes.

Bean Curd and 'Three Treasure' Soup *(for 4-6 people)*

2 cakes bean curd
1½ tbs lard
750 ml-1 litre (1½-2 pints) good stock
1 stock cube
1½ tbs dry sherry
salt and pepper (to taste)
1½ tbs cornflour (blended in 5-6 tbs water)
2 tbs minced ham

Three Treasures
   5-6 tbs shrimps (fresh or frozen)
   12.5-15 cm (5-6 in) sections of cucumber (or use 3 tbs
      green peas)
   5-6 medium size Chinese dried mushrooms

Preparation
Cut bean curd into 20-30 cubes. Soak mushrooms in warm
water for 20-30 mins, remove stalks and cut each cap into
10-12 pieces (square where possible). Cut cucumber,
including skin, into 4-6 mm (⅙-¼ in) cubes.

Cooking and Serving
Heat lard in the wok. When hot, add shrimps and
mushrooms. Stir them over medium heat for 1½ mins.
Add stock, stock cube, cucumber and bean curd. Bring
contents to boil, reduce heat to a simmer and cook gently
for 6-7 mins. Add sherry and salt and pepper to taste and
pour in the cornflour mixture. Stir until the soup thickens.
Sprinkle the top of the soup with ham and serve as in the
previous recipes.

Marrow and Spare-rib Soup *(for 4-6 people)*

   400 g (1 lb) spare-ribs
   400 g (1 lb) section of marrow
   1½ tbs lard
   1 litre (2 pints) good stock
   ½ chicken stock cube
   salt and pepper (to taste)

Preparation
Chop spare-ribs into 5 cm (2 in) sections. Peel marrow and
cut into 5 cm × 4 cm (2 in × 1½ in) pieces. Parboil spare-
ribs in boiling water for 7-8 mins and the marrow for 4
mins and drain.

Cooking and Serving

Heat lard in the wok. When hot, add the spare-ribs and stir-fry over medium heat for 3-4 mins. Add stock and bring contents to a gentle boil. Simmer for 20 mins. Add marrow and stock cube. Simmer for 15 mins. Adjust for seasoning with salt and pepper. Serve the soup as in the previous recipes.

Sliced Fish in Vinegar Pepper-Pot Soup *(for 4-6 people)*

200-300 g (½-¾ lb) filleted fish (sole, place cod, halibut, bream etc.)
1½ tsp salt
½ tbs cornflour
½ egg white
2 stalks spring onion
4 tbs vinegar
1 tbs soya sauce
2 tbs white wine
¼ tsp freshly-ground black pepper
750 ml-1 litre (1½-2 pints) good stock
½ stock cube

Preparation

Cut fish roughly into 5 cm × 2.5 cm (2 in × 1 in) slices. Sprinkle and rub with salt and cornflour. Leave for 15 mins and wet with egg white. Cut spring onions into 6 mm (¼ in) shavings. Mix vinegar, soya sauce, wine and pepper in cup or bowl.

Cooking and Serving

Heat stock in the wok. When it starts to boil, lower the fish piece by piece into the boiling stock. When contents start to re-boil, add the contents from the bowl and the stock cube. Stir the contents gently a few times. Simmer for 2 mins and sprinkle the contents with spring onion. Serve as in the previous recipes. This is a soup with considerable impact.

Fish Head and Tail Soup with Bean Curd *(for 6 people)*

2 rashers bacon
1 medium onion
2 cakes bean curd
1½ tbs lard
3 slices root-ginger
400 g (1 lb) fish heads and tails
1 litre (2 pints) good stock
1 chicken stock cube
2 tbs vinegar
1 tbs soya sauce
2 tbs white wine or sherry
1 tsp salt

Preparation
Cut bacon into shreds, cut onion into thin slices. Cut each bean curd cake into 20-24 pieces.

Cooking and Serving
Heat lard in the wok. Add onion, ginger and bacon. Stir-fry them over high heat for 2 mins. Add fish heads and tails. Turn them in the lard and fat (from the bacon) for 1 min. Pour in the stock and add stock cube, vinegar, soya sauce, wine or sherry and salt. When contents start to boil, reduce heat to simmer and cook gently for 10 mins. Add the bean curd and simmer gently for another 10 mins and serve in a large soup bowl or tureen for the diners to help themselves from with a communal ladle. This is a quite substantial soup and is treated as a 'semi-soup' main course on the Chinese domestic table and is much loved by the hungry mouths which frequently surround it.

Rice Dishes

Rice is seldom cooked in the wok in China, except as 'fried rice' which is often cooked from plain boiled or steamed rice which has been left over from the previous day; such rice can also be re-heated by tossing in the wok and be made into a kind of 'hot salad', with some infusion of stock and the addition of one or two ingredients; usually a fresh green vegetable and a cooked meat or two (often the left-overs of main course dishes from previous meals) resulting in simple dishes which are serviceable and appealing to the palate. In all such cases, the rice used is always cooked rice and since the cooking of rice has often, for some reason in the west, grown into a subject of controversy, I shall reiterate here the simplest way in which rice is cooked by the Chinese, before the arrival of the electric rice cooker (thermostatically controlled and automatic) which to the majority of the Chinese is an unnecessary piece of modern gadgetry.

Boiled Rice (for 4-6 or more people)

500 ml (1 pint) rice
750 ml (1½ pints) water

Preparation and Cooking

Wash and rinse rice with two changes of water, and drain. Place the rice in a heavy saucepan. Add the water. Bring the contents to boil and reduce heat to very low (insert an asbestos sheet under the pan, if you have one), leaving the rice to cook as gently as possible for 10 mins under cover. Do not uncover. Turn the heat off and leave rice to stand on the cooker to cook in the residual heat for the next 10 mins when the rice should be quite dry and well-cooked and ready for use.

Basic Fried Rice *(for 2-3 people)*

1 medium-sized onion
2-3 rashers bacon
1 tsp salt
2-3 eggs
2-3 tbs vegetable oil
1 tbs butter
300-400 g (¾-1 lb) or 2-3 bowls cooked rice
2-3 tbs green peas (fresh or frozen)
1 tbs soya sauce

Preparation

Cut onion into thin slices and bacon into thin strips. Add salt to eggs and beat with a fork for 10-12 seconds.

Cooking and Serving

Heat oil in the wok. Add onion and bacon. Stir-fry over medium heat for 2 mins. Push them to one side of the wok and add butter to the other side. When it has melted pour in the egg. Stir the egg a couple of times and leave to cook for a minute. When the egg is about set, pour in the rice, peas and soya sauce and turn and scramble it with the other contents of the wok until the ingredients are evenly mixed. Leave to cook over low heat for 2½ more mins, when the Fried Rice should be almost ready to serve. Turn, stir and scramble once more and serve. This simple, lightly-fried Fried Rice is what is normally served when you have one to two other savoury dishes to serve with the bulk food (rice or fried rice).

If no other dishes are available to serve with the bulk food the Fried Rice is generally made fancier, that is, with more ingredients added. Such fancy fried rice should be eaten with a soup, hot tea or with a long drink such as beer or lager.

Fried Rice with Diced Meat and Mushrooms *(for 2-3 people)*

    100 g (¼ lb) button mushrooms
    100-200 g (¼-½ lb) cooked meat (pork, lamb, beef, chicken scraped from joints or carcass)
    1½ tbs vegetable oil
    ½ tbs butter
    1½ tbs soya sauce
    ½ tsp sugar
    400 g (1 lb) Basic Fried Rice

Preparation
Wash mushrooms, remove and discard stalks and dice caps into 6 mm (¼ in) cubes. Dice meat into roughly similar cubes.

Cooking and Serving
Heat oil in the wok. When hot, add mushrooms and stir-fry over high heat for 2 mins. Reduce heat to medium. Add butter and meat, sprinkle contents with soya sauce and sugar. Stir and turn them together for 1½ mins. Add the Fried Rice. Stir and turn them together with the other contents of the wok. Leave contents to heat through for the next 1½ - 2 mins. Stir and turn once more and serve in individual bowls or well-heated serving plates, one for each diner at the table. What is left in the wok (if any) will keep hot on the cooker (away from heat) for a few minutes.

Fried Rice with Shrimps and Bamboo-Shoots *(for 2-4 people)*

    400 g (1 lb) Basic Fried Rice

3-4 tbs fresh or frozen shrimps
2 stalks spring onion
75-100 g (3-4 oz) bamboo-shoots

Preparation, Cooking and Serving

Repeat the previous recipe. Dice bamboo-shoots into 4 mm
(⅙ in) cubes and cut spring onions into 6 mm (¼ in)
segments or shavings. Add them into the pan, short stir-
frying when meat is added with ¾ tbs of additional oil.
Turn and toss them with all the other ingredients and serve
the finished dish as in the previous recipe. The inclusion of
shrimps adds a new dimension to the savouriness of the
dish.

Hot-Tossed 'Rice Salad' with Greens and Ham *(for 2-4 people)*

300 g (¾ lb) spring greens or cabbage
100-300 g (½-¾ lb) gammon (or ham)
2 tbs vegetable oil
1 tsp salt
1 tbs lard (or butter)
400 g (1 lb) cooked rice (hot or cold)
250 ml (½ pint) good stock (strengthened with ½
    chicken stock cube)

Preparation

Cut greens into 2.5-4 cm (1-1½ in) slices (after removing
tougher stems and discoloured leaves) and cut gammon or
ham into 2.5 mm × 6 mm (1 in × ¼ in) pieces.

Cooking and Serving

Heat oil in the wok. When hot, add the greens, sprinkle
with salt and turn over medium heat for 2 mins. Add the
lard and gammon and turn and mix them with the
other ingredients in the wok for 1½ mins. Add the cooked

rice, turn and mix evenly with the gammon and greens. Pour the stock evenly over the contents of the wok. Leave to cook gently over low heat for 10 mins. Serve on plates or in individual bowls to be eaten on its own or with other savoury dishes. The above quantity should be sufficient for 4-5 people if served with one savoury dish and soup.

Hot-Tossed 'Rice Salad' with French Beans (or Broccoli) and Soya Pork (or beef, lamb or chicken) *(for 3-5 people)*

300 g (¾ lb) French Beans (or broccoli)
300 g (¾ lb) soya braised meat (cooked but cold)
2 tbs vegetable oil
1 tsp salt
½ tbs lard (or butter)
400 g (1 lb) cooked rice
250 ml (½ pint) good stock (strengthened with ½ chicken stock cube)

Preperation

Top and tail the beans and cut each slantwise into 2.5 cm (1 in) sections. Cut cold braised pork into approximately 12 mm-2.5 cm (½-1 in) pieces.

Cooking and Serving

Heat oil in the wok. Add beans, sprinkle with salt and stir-fry over medium heat for 2 mins. Add the lard and pork, stir them together with the beans for 1 min. Add the rice, turn and toss it, to mix evenly with other contents of the wok. Pour the stock evenly over the mixed ingredients. Place a cover over the wok and leave the contents to simmer gently together for 10 mins. Turn the contents over once more and serve on well-heated individual plates or in bowls. The above quantity should be sufficient for 3-5 people, with one savoury dish and soup.

Hot-Tossed 'Rice Salad' with Salt Beef (or pork), Cauliflower and Brussels Sprouts *(for 3-5 people)*

1 small cauliflower
100 g (¼ lb) Brussels sprouts
300 g (¾ lb) salt beef (or pork)
2 tbs vegetable oil
1 tsp salt
400 g (1 lb) cooked rice
1 tbs lard (or butter)
250 ml (½ pint) good stock (strengthened with ½ chicken stock cube)
½ tbs soya sauce

Preparation
Break cauliflower into small individual flowerets. Cut each sprout in half (or into quarters, depending on size) removing discoloured leaves. Cut beef into 6 mm (¼ in) cubes.

Cooking and Serving
Heat oil in the wok. Add the vegetables, sprinkle with salt. Stir-fry them over medium heat for 2 mins. Add beef, rice and lard to mix with the vegetables. When they are evenly mixed, pour the stock in evenly. Bring contents to boil. Place a lid over the wok and reduce heat to very low. Leave contents to simmer very gently for 10 mins. Serve as in the previous recipe, in well-heated bowls or on plates. Sprinkle the top of each dish with a small amount of soya sauce.

Hot-Tossed 'Rice Salad' with Fish and Salt Fish *(for 3-5 people)*

300 g (¾ lb) filleted fish (cod, halibut, haddock, bream, mullet etc.)

200 g (½ lb) salt fish (dried squid, kipper or smoked haddock etc.)
1 medium onion
2 stalks spring onion
3 garlic cloves
2 tbs vegetable oil
1 tbs lard (or butter)
400 g (1 lb) cooked rice
250 ml (½ pint) good stock (strengthened with ½ chicken stock cube)
1 tsp salt
1 tbs soya sauce

Preparation
Cut fresh fish into 2.5 cm (1 in) pieces and salt fish into 12 mm (½ in) pieces (after removing bones). Cut onion into thin slices, and spring onions into 12 mm (½ in) sections. Crush and mince garlic coarsely.

Cooking and Serving
Heat oil and lard in the wok. Add onion and garlic. Stir-fry them over medium heat for 1½ mins. Add fresh fish and turn it with the other ingredients for 2 mins. Add the rice and salt fish. Turn and mix them evenly with the other contents of the wok. Pour the stock evenly over the fish and rice. Reduce heat and leave to simmer under cover very gently for 10 mins. Open the lid and sprinkle the contents evenly with spring onion, salt and soya sauce. Serve by dividing onto plates or in individual bowls.

Hot Tossed 'Rice Salad' with a Variety of Selected Vegetables (for 4-5 people)

2 small young carrots
1 aubergine
2 stalks leeks

1 stick celery
1 small green cabbage
1 medium onion
1 cake bean curd (optional)
2 medium tomatoes
2½ tbs vegetable oil
1½ tbs lard (or butter)
4 tbs sweetcorn
1½ tsp salt
400 g (1 lb) cooked rice
250 ml (½ pint) good stock (strengthened with 1 chicken
    stock cube)
1 tsp sesame oil
2 tbs soya sauce

Preparation
Cut carrots and aubergine into 12 mm (½ in) cubes, leeks
and celery diagonally into 12 mm (½ in) sections, cabbage
into 2.5 cm (1 in) slices and onion into thin slices. Dice
bean curd into 12 mm (½ in) cubes. Chop the tomatoes.

Cooking
Heat oil in the wok. Add bean curd, onion and carrots to
turn gently in the hot oil for 2½ mins. Add lard and all the
other vegetables. Sprinkle with salt and turn and stir them
over high heat for 2 mins. Add the rice to mix evenly with
the other ingredients. Pour the stock evenly over the
contents of the wok. Reduce heat and simmer very gently
under cover for 10 mins.

Serving
Serve by dividing the contents of the wok into 4-5 serving
plates or individual bowls. Sprinkle the top of the contents
of the bowls or plates with the sesame oil and soya sauce.

Hot-Tossed 'Rice Salad' with Minced Meat and Assorted Vegetables *(for 3-5 people)*

1 medium onion
2 garlic cloves
300 g (¾ lb) any assortment of vegetables (cabbage, cauliflower, carrots, radish, marrow, courgettes, aubergine, peas etc.)
2 tbs vegetable oil
200-300 g (½-¾ lb) minced meat (pork or beef)
1½ tbs lard (or butter)
2 tbs mixed pickles (or chopped gherkin)
400 g (1 lb) cooked rice
250 ml (½ pint) good stock (strengthened with ½ chicken stock cube)
1 tsp salt
2 tbs soya sauce

Preparation

Cut onion into thin slices, crush and chop garlic. Cut vegetables roughly into 2.5-4 cm (1 in-1½ in) size pieces.

Cooking and Serving

Heat oil in the wok. When hot, add onion and garlic. Stir over high heat for 1 min. Add minced meat. Stir and turn them together for 2 mins, add all the vegetables, lard and pickles. Stir and turn them all together for 3 mins. Add the rice to mix evenly with all the other ingredients. Pour the stock evenly over the contents of the wok and sprinkle them with salt and half the soya sauce. Reduce heat to very low and simmer very gently for 10 mins. Serve by dividing the contents into 3-5 serving bowls or plates and sprinkle them with the balance of the soya sauce. Serve as before.

Noodle Dishes

Noodles are cooked and consumed in China mainly in four forms; fried (chow mein), in sauce, in soup or tossed with shredded vegetables and a meat sauce. All four forms of noodles can be, and are, cooked traditionally in the wok. The recipes below illustrate styles of dishes.

Viewed objectively, the principal difference between Chinese noodles and Italian spaghetti and vermicelli dishes lies in that Chinese noodle dishes are usually 'double decker' affairs, that is, the noodles are initially boiled and drained and are served after having been not only tossed with meat and sauce in the wok, but also laden with a good layer of quick-fried garnish (the garnish being the 'upper deck'). The Italian versions are largely 'single decker' affairs where the savoury ingredients to be served with the pasta are mixed and tossed with it at the table. In the case of noodles served in soups, the Italians usually serve their pastas, which are cut short, floating in the soup with the other ingredients, whilst the Chinese would serve their noodles in full length, curled in a loose bundle submerged in the soup or sauce. The great physical enjoyment of eating noodles in this form is to 'absorb' the noodles with the soup or sauce, a process which is half eating and half drinking. The consumption of the 'garnish' which can sometimes be quite chunky pieces of meat or vegetable is considered just a 'diversion'. The connoisseur's enjoyment lies fundamentally in 'absorbing' and tucking into the noodles themselves.

FRIED NOODLES OR CHOW MEIN

Chow Mein (or 'Fried Noodles') with Shredded Meat and Vegetables (for 3-4 people)

> 400-600 g (1-1½ lb) Chinese noodles (or spaghetti)
> 1 medium onion
> 300 g (¾ lb) meat (pork, chicken, beef or lamb)
> 2½ tbs vegetable oil
> ½ tsp salt
> 100 g (½ lb) bean sprouts
> 2½ tbs soya sauce

For Garnish
> 2 stalks spring onion
> 6 large button mushrooms
> 4 Chinese dried mushrooms (optional)
> 1½ tbs lard (or butter)
> 1½ tbs dry sherry
> 3 tbs good stock

Preparation
Boil Chinese noodles for 7-8 mins or spaghetti for 18 mins and drain. Rinse under running water. Cut onion into thin slices and meat into matchstick shreds. Cut spring onion into 2.5 cm (1 in) sections, button mushrooms into thin slices. Soak Chinese mushrooms in warm water for 30 mins, remove stalks and cut caps into shreds.

Cooking and Serving
Heat oil in the wok. When hot, add onion and meat, sprinkle them with salt and stir-fry over high heat for 2 mins. Add bean sprouts, sprinkle with ½ tbs soya sauce and continue to stir for a further 2 mins. Remove half the ingredients from the wok and put aside. Add the noodles into the wok, sprinkle with 1 tbs of soya sauce and turn

and mix them with the ingredients in the wok. Reduce heat and allow the noodles to heat through (about 4-5 mins), turning them slowly now and then. Remove all the noodles etc. from the wok into a well-heated deep-sided serving dish.

Wipe the wok with a damp cloth. Add lard. When it has melted, add the mushrooms and dried mushrooms. Stir them over high heat for 1½ mins. Return the ingredients (meat etc.) which had been removed from the wok and set aside earlier. Add the sherry, spring onion, stock and remainder of the soya sauce. Stir all the contents together still over high heat for 2 mins. Ladle and spread the contents over the top of the noodles in the serving dish and pour the gravy from the wok over them. Serve by placing the dish at the centre of the table for the diners to help themselves from.

Seafood 'Chow Mein' *(for 3-4 people)*

400-600 g (1-1½ lb) Chinese noodles (or spaghetti)
2 medium onions
3-4 rashers bacon
1 stick celery
2 slices root-ginger
2-4 tbs crab meat
1 small tin (100 g or 4 oz) clams (or 6 small oysters or mussels)
1½ tbs dried shrimps
2½ tbs vegetable oil
1 tsp salt
2 tbs soya sauce

For Garnish

2 garlic cloves
6-8 large 'Pacific' prawns or 2-4 scallops (optional)
2 stalks spring onion
1 tbs lard (or butter)

3 tbs good stock
2 tbs dry sherry

Preparation

Boil noodles for 6-7 mins (or spaghetti for 18 mins) and drain. Rinse under running water. Cut onions into thin slices, bacon and celery and ginger into matchstick shreds. Flake crab meat. If using oysters or mussels, remove from shells after poaching in boiling water for 3 mins. Soak dried shrimps in warm water for 30 mins and drain. Crush and chop garlic. Shell the prawns (or scallops). Chop spring onions.

Cooking and Serving

Heat oil in the wok. When hot, add onion, ginger, bacon, celery and dried shrimps. Stir-fry them over high heat for 2 mins. Add crab meat and clams (or oysters or mussels). Sprinkle them with salt and continue to stir-fry for 1½ mins. Add the noodles to stir and turn with the other ingredients in the wok. Reduce heat to low to allow the noodles to heat through for 4-5 mins, turning the noodles gently now and then and sprinkling them with 2 tbs soya sauce.

Remove the well-mixed contents of the wok and place them in a large well-heated serving dish. Wipe the wok with a damp cloth and return it to the heat. Add lard, spring onion, garlic into the wok. Turn heat high and stir the ingredients around a few times. Add the prawns or scallops. Continue to turn and stir-fry for 1 min. Pour in the stock and sherry. When the contents begin to boil, turn and stir the contents around for 15 seconds. Spoon or ladle the contents over as garnish on top of the noodles in the serving dish. Pour the gravy evenly over the dish and serve by placing the dish at the centre of the table for the diners to help themselves from.

Vegetable 'Chow Mein' (for 3-4 people)

400-600 g (1-1½ lb) noodles (or spaghetti)
1 stick celery
2 small young carrots
10 cm (4 in) section cucumber
4 medium Chinese dried mushrooms
5-6 medium button mushrooms
100 g (¼ lb) young spinach
2 stalks spring onion
2 garlic cloves
50-75 g (2-3 oz) bamboo shoots
3 tbs vegetable oil
5-6 tbs bean sprouts
2 tbs mixed pickles
4 tbs soya sauce
1½ tbs lard
4-5 tbs canned miniature corn (optional)
2½ tbs stock
1 tbs dry sherry
2 tsp sesame oil

Preparation
Boil noodles (or spaghetti), drain and rinse as in the previous recipe. Cut celery, carrots, cucumber (including skin) into double matchstick strips. Soak dried mushrooms in warm water for 20 mins. Remove stalks and cut into similar shreds. Cut button mushrooms into thin slices. Remove the tougher stems and any discoloured leaves from the spinach, wash thoroughly and tear into 7.5 cm (3 in) pieces. Cut spring onions into 5 cm (2 in) sections, crush and chop garlic. Slice bamboo shoots.

Cooking and Serving
Heat oil in the wok. When hot, add celery, carrots, bamboo shoots, dried mushrooms and stir-fry them over

high heat for 2 mins. Add bean sprouts, cucumber, pickles and sprinkle them all with 1½ tbs soya sauce. Stir and turn them around in the wok for 1 min. Reduce heat, allowing the noodles to heat through for about 3-4 mins, turning the contents over gently now and then. Remove the contents into a well-heated deep-sided serving dish.

Wipe the wok with a damp cloth. Add lard. When hot, add the spinach, garlic and mushrooms. Stir them over high heat for 2 mins. Add the corn, balance of soya sauce, stock and sherry. Continue to stir-fry for a further minute. Sprinkle the contents with sesame oi! and ladle them as garnish over the top of the noodles etc., in the large serving dish. Place the dish at the centre of the table for the diners to divide and help themselves from. All 'Chow Mein' should be eaten hot, soon after leaving the wok.

NOODLES IN SAUCE

'Noodles in sauce' differ from 'Chow Mein' or 'Fried Noodles' mainly in that they are prepared together with the gravy of a long-cooked braised or stewed meat and the meat is in this case in chunky pieces quickly stir-fried (sometimes with some vegetables) and placed on top of the noodles as a 'garnish'. The gravy from the meat is converted into the 'sauce' simply by adding 375-500 ml (¾-1 pint) of good stock into the stew (after lifting out the pieces of meat) and strengthening it with a small amount of soya sauce and wine and thickening it with some cornflour. The noodles which have previously been par-boiled and drained are then cooked in this sauce for a short period of time (3-5 mins) and served in large individual bowls decorated or garnished with a layer of braised meat and any vegetables which had been quick-fried with it. This does not mean, however, that 'noodles in sauce' cannot be prepared without stewed or braised meat. Indeed, all

Chow Meins or 'Fried Noodles' can be converted into quiet, acceptable and palatable 'noodles in sauce' simply by adding a quantity of good stock into the wok to be cooked with the meat and vegetables which are stir-fried in it (after removing ¼-⅓ of it for the eventual garnish) and leaving them to simmer for some 10 mins and thickening it with some blended cornflour and strengthening the 'sauce' by the addition of a judicous amount of soya sauce and some wine or sherry (equivalent to Chinese rice-wine called 'Yellow Wine'). The noodles should then be added and cooked in this hot and tasty 'concoction' for a matter of 4-5 mins before being served with the 'garnish'. But ideally 'noodles in sauce' is best prepared when there is a large pot or casserole of braised or stewed meat available.

The great enjoyment of eating 'noodles in sauce' lies principally in 'absorbing' (or sucking in the noodles) from a bowl of tasty sauce, a sensation not readily available in western eating (because most of your main dishes are eaten from a plate rather than from a bowl).

Since long-cooked braised meat is used in the cooking of 'noodles in sauce' I shall just mention very shortly here how these meat dishes are usually cooked before treating them at greater length in a later chapter. Chinese long-cooked dishes are usually cooked in a closed heat-proof bowl, earthenware pot or casserole which is steamed or stood in a panful of boiling water which is kept at a simmer over a period of 2-3 or more hours. This can conveniently be done in a wok by filling it with 1.25-1.5 litres (2½-3 pints) of water and bringing the latter to the boil. The pot or basin containing the meat and flavouring ingredients is then placed to stand in the gently boiling water, and covered with a lid or tinfoil or grease-proof paper tied firmly on. A deep lid is then placed to close the top of the wok. When meat or any other food materials are slow-cooked in this manner for 2-3 hours or more (the water in the wok is replenished every now and then), they generally become extremely tender; and if suitable flavouring materials are added at the outset with a reasonable amount of water or stock, the resultant gravy should be plentiful and extremely tasty.

Noodles in Sauce with Long-Braised Beef *(for 3-4 people)*

400-600 g (1-1½ lb) Chinese noodles (or spaghetti)
2 garlic cloves
200 g (½ lb) spinach
400 g (1 lb) long-braised soya beef (which has been previously cooked for 2-3 hours in ample gravy)
500 ml (1 pint) good stock
1 chicken stock cube
1½ tbs soya sauce
3-4 tbs sherry or white wine
1½ tbs cornflour (blended in 4-5 tbs water)
1½ tbs vegetable oil
1 tbs lard (or butter)
2 stalks spring onion
½ tsp salt

Preparation

Boil noodles for 4-5 mins (or spaghetti for 10 mins) and drain, rinse under running water. Crush and chop garlic, remove tougher stems from the spinach and cut into 5-7.5 cm (2-3 in) slices.

Cooking and Serving

Put beef (ready-cut into bite-size pieces) aside and pour all the gravy into the wok. Add stock and stock cube. Bring contents to boil. Add soya sauce, sherry or wine and blended cornflour. Stir until the liquid thickens somewhat. Add the noodles and leave contents to simmer gently for 4-5 mins. Divide and pour the noodles and sauce into 3 large bowls.

Wipe the wok with a damp cloth. Add oil and lard. As soon as the oil/fat is very hot, add garlic and spinach. Stir-fry them together over high heat for 2 mins. Add beef and chopped spring onions and salt and turn them with the beef for a further 2 mins. Serve them on top of the noodles in the bowls as garnish. Serve the bowlfuls of noodles to the diners who should be equipped with both chopsticks and a spoon. The consumption of such a bowlful of 'noodles in sauce' is invariably enjoyable and most suitable for a cold day.

Noodles in Sauce with Long-Braised Pork (for 3-5 people)

400-600 g (1-1½ lb) Chinese noodles (or spaghetti)
2 garlic cloves
2-3 stalks celery
600 g (1½-lb) long-braised soya pork with skin
500 ml (1 pint) good stock
1 chicken stock cube
1½ tbs soya sauce
3-4 tbs sherry or white wine
½ tsp salt
1½ tbs cornflour (blended in 4-5 tbs water)
1½ tbs vegetable oil
1 tbs lard (or butter)
2 stalks spring onion

Preparation
Boil noodles for 4-5 mins (or spaghetti for 12 mins). Drain and rinse under running water. Crush and chop garlic, cut celery diagonally into 5 cm (2 in) sections.

Cooking and Serving
Put pork aside after cutting into large bite-size pieces (including skin). Pour all the gravy into the wok. Add stock and stock cube. Bring contents to the boil. Add soya

sauce, sherry or wine, salt and blended cornflour. Stir until the liquid thickens. Add the noodles and leave to simmer gently for 4-5 mins. Divide and pour the noodles and sauce into 3-5 large bowls (1 for each diner).

Wipe the wok with a damp cloth. Add oil and lard. As soon as the oil/fat is hot, add garlic and celery. Stir them over high heat for 1½ mins. Add pork pieces and chopped spring onions. Turn and stir them together for 2 mins. Serve them on top of the noodles in the bowls as garnish. The 3-5 diners should all be equipped with chopsticks and spoons to tackle their individual bowl of noodles, which are heavily garnished and submerged in ample sauce.

Noodles in Sauce with Seafood *(for 3-5 people)*

1 tbs dried shrimps
200 g (½ lb) lean and fat pork
1 medium onion
2 stalks spring onion
2 slices root-ginger
2 garlic cloves
400-600 g (1-1½ lb) Chinese noodles (or spaghetti)
2½ tbs vegetable oil
4-5 tbs prawns (peeled)
2-3 tbs clam meat
3-4 tbs crab meat
4-5 tbs mussels or oysters (shelled)
125 ml (¼ pint) pork gravy (gravy or long-cooked soya pork)
500 ml (1 pint) good stock
½ chicken stock cube
1½ tbs cornflour (blended in 4 tbs water)
1 tbs lard
½ tbs soya sauce
3 tbs dry sherry or white wine

Preparation

Soak dried shrimps in warm water for 30 mins and drain. Cut pork into shreds. Cut onion into thin slices and spring onions into 2.5 cm (1 in) sections. Shred ginger. Crush and chop garlic. Boil and drain noodles or spaghetti as in the previous recipe.

Cooking and Serving

Heat oil in the wok. Add ginger, onion, dried shrimps and pork. Stir-fry them over high heat for 2 mins. Add prawns, clams, crab, mussels or oysters. Stir-fry them together for 2 mins. Remove half the ingredients from the wok and put aside. Add the gravy, stock and stock cube into the wok. Bring contents to boil. Stir them around for 2 mins and add blended cornflour. Continue to stir until the liquid thickens. Add the noodles or spaghetti and leave them to simmer in the sauce for 4-5 mins. Divide the noodles and sauce into 3-5 bowls.

Wipe the wok with a damp cloth. Add lard. When it has melted, add garlic and spring onions. Stir them around a couple of times and add all the seafood and shredded pork which had been put aside. Sprinkle them with soya sauce and sherry. Stir them around in the wok for 1 min. Spoon the contents over the top of each bowl of noodles as garnish. The noodles are therefore submerged in sauce and garnished with quick-fried food. Such noodles are often unbelievably delicious.

SOUP NOODLES (OR NOODLES IN SOUP)

'Soup noodles' are what is often called nowadays 'Main Course Soup', something which will constitute on its own a large snack meal. 'Soup noodles' are often prepared and served in China when there are not many other ingredients available, except for noodles and stock and the bits and pieces which are generally found lying about in the kitchen. The following is one of these simple recipes made from 'bits and pieces'.

Basic 'Bits and Pieces' Soup Noodles (for 3-4 people)

2 rashers of bacon (or 100 g (¼ lb) ham)
2-3 medium mushrooms
100 g (½ lb) scrapings of shredded chicken meat (from a cooked chicken) or shredded pork or beef or lamb (from leftover roasts)
5 cm (2 in) section of gherkin
200 g (½ lb) spring greens (or spinach)
400-600 g (1-1½ lb) Chinese noodles (or spaghetti)
1 medium onion
2 tbs vegetable oil
1 tsp salt
1 litre (2 pints) meat and bone stock (can be made from poultry carcass or pig's trotters)
1½ chicken stock cubes
1½ tbs soya sauce
1 tbs lard (or butter)
2 stalks spring onion
1-2 tbs dry sherry

Preparation

Cut bacon, meat, mushrooms, gherkin and greens all into matchstick shreds (after discarding tough stalks, stems and rinds). Cut spring onions into 2.5 cm (1 in) sections. Boil noodles for 6 mins or spaghetti for 12 mins. Rinse and drain. Cut onion into very thin slices.

Cooking and Serving

Heat oil in the wok. When hot, add onion, bacon to stir together for 1 min. Add shredded meat, mushrooms, gherkin and greens. Stir and turn them over high heat for

1½ mins. Sprinkle them with salt and continue to stir-fry for 1½ mins. Remove half the contents of the wok and put aside. Pour the stock into the wok, add stock cube and ½ tbs soya sauce and bring the contents to the boil. Stir the contents around a few times and add the noodles. Leave the contents to simmer in the wok for the next 5-6 mins. Divide the soup and noodles into 3-4 large serving bowls.

Wipe the wok with a damp cloth and add lard. When the lard has melted, add spring onions, balance of soya sauce and the ingredients which had been taken out of the wok and put aside. Stir-fry them all over high heat for 1 min. Ladle them out and place them on top of the 3-4 bowls of 'soup noodles' as garnish.

All 'soup noodles' are very warming and good for the winter, especially when you do not have many food ingredients about.

'Soup noodles' can, of course, be made with the same ingredients and food materials used in the 'Noodles in Sauce' recipes, even if there were only half the flavouring and garnishing ingredients available. The only thing which will need to be done is to increase the amount of stock used to 1 litre (2 pints) and the stock cubes to 1½ cubes and eliminate the use of cornflour for thickening. Therefore, in the case of:-

Soup Noodles with Long-Braised Beef *(for 3-4 people)*

Use the recipe for Noodles in Sauce with Long-Braised Beef (see page 88) but use half the beef to cook with the stock and noodles (par-boiled) for 6-7 mins. Stir-fry the other half of the beef, with spinach, in vegetable oil and only half as much lard (or butter). This second half of the beef and ingredients which had been shortly stir-fried are then used as garnish or toppings for the noodles and soup which had been divided into serving bowls.

Soup Noodles with Long-Braised Pork *(for 3-4 people)*

Use the recipe for Noodles in Sauce with Long-Braised Pork (see page 89). Divide the pork into two halves. Use the first half to cook with the noodles (ready par-boiled) with 1 litre (2 pints) of stock and 1½ chicken stock cubes added; use the other half to stir-fry with celery, spring onion and other ingredients with oil and half the amount of lard, for a couple of minutes and use the stir-fried foods as garnish or topping for the noodles and soup which had been divided into the 3-4 serving bowls.

Soup Noodles with Shrimps and Minced Meat *(for 3-4 people)*

    400-600 g (1-1½ lb) noodles or spaghetti
    1 medium onion
    1 small gherkin
    2 garlic cloves
    1½ tbs vegetable oil
    200 g (½ lb) minced meat (pork or beef)
    1 tsp salt
    100 g (¼ lb) shrimps (frozen)
    1 litre (2 pints) good stock
    1½ chicken stock cubes
    1 small bunch watercress
    1½ tbs lard (or butter)
    100 g (¼ lb) green peas (frozen or fresh)
    1½ tbs soya sauce
    2 tbs sherry or wine

Preparation
Parboil the noodles, rinse and drain as in the recipes for 'soup noodles'. Cut onion and gherkin into thin slices and chop coarsely. Crush and chop garlic.

Cooking and Serving

Heat oil in the wok. Add onion and minced meat. Sprinkle with salt and stir-fry over high heat for 2 mins. Add gherkin and shrimps. Continue to stir-fry for 2 mins, remove two-thirds of the contents and put aside. Pour the stock into the wok, add stock cubes, watercress, noodles and bring to the boil. Reduce heat and leave the contents to simmer for 5-6 mins. Divide the noodles, watercress and soup into 3-4 large serving bowls.

Wipe the wok with a damp cloth. Add lard. When it has melted, add garlic and green peas. Stir them over high heat for 1½ mins. Add the minced meat etc. which had previously been taken out of the wok. Sprinkle the contents with soya sauce. Stir-fry the mixed contents of the wok for 1½ mins over high heat. Sprinkle them with sherry or wine and spoon them out and place them as a garnish on top of the noodles and soup in the 3-4 individual bowls. This is a fairly inexpensive yet satisfying dish. Its quantity can be augmented to serve an even larger number of people by simply increasing the noodles or spaghetti used without having necessarily to increase any of the other ingredients used. A cheap snack meal.

Before concluding this section on 'soup noodles', it should be noted that all soup dishes can be converted into 'soup noodles' simply by adding parboiled noodles which had been drained into the soup for a few minutes of simmering together. For westerners, however, because they are unused to food with small bones (especially fish bones) the soups where fish is used as the main ingredient for the soup should be avoided. Furthermore, as westerners are appreciative of Chinese foods which are highly savoury and since noodles are in themselves bland in flavour, the flavour of soups which are used as a base for soup noodles should be intensified by adding 1 tbs of soya sauce, 1 extra chicken stock cube and 1 tbs of chopped spring onions. And, if dried mushrooms are available, these (4-6) should be added to simmer in the soup together with the mushroom water after 30 mins of soaking. The making of soups in China is not unlike concocting a 'savoury cocktail', anything which harmonizes with the principal flavour of the soup can be added to improve the appeal of the dish.

Fish Dishes

Fish can be cooked in the wok as readily and conveniently as meat; perhaps even more so, since most fish does not require long cooking and the wok is, in the main, an instrument for 'instant' cooking, although, as I already demonstrated in the previous recipes, it can be used in braising; and in the recipes to follow I will show how it can also be used for steaming.

QUICK-FRIED AND BRAISED FISH DISHES

Quick-fried and Braised Fish with Ginger and Spring Onion (for 4-6 people to be served with rice and one or two other dishes)

400-600 g (1-1½ lb) chunky fish (ie fish in large cuts –
    cod, conger, halibut, haddock, sea bream, shad,
    salmon etc.)
1½ tsp salt
1½ tbs cornflour
2½ tbs vegetable oil
3 slices root-ginger
3 stalks spring onion
2½ tbs soya sauce
1 tbs vinegar
2 tbs dry sherry (or wine)
1 tsp sugar
1 tbs lard (or butter)
2 tbs stock

Preparation

Cut fish into 5 cm × 4 cm (2 in × 1½ in) pieces. Sprinkle and rub with salt, cornflour and ¾ tbs oil. Leave to season for 15 mins. Shred ginger and cut spring onions into short shavings. Divide each into two parts. Use one half to mix together with soya sauce, vinegar, sherry or wine and sugar in a bowl into a 'sauce'.

Cooking and Serving

Heat lard and remaining oil in the wok. Add the remaining half of the ginger and onion to stir-fry in the fat and oil for 1 min. Add the fish into the hot fat/oil in the wok piece by piece. After a minute's static-frying turn the pieces around and fry them for a further 2 mins, 1 min on each side. Pour the stock and 'sauce' over the pieces of fish. Turn the fish a few times in the 'sauce' which should start to boil. Place a lid over the wok, and leave contents to simmer for 3 mins. Serve by transferring the pieces of fish into a bowl or deep-sided dish and pour the gravy from the wok over them. When consumed with rice the majority of rice-eaters find this fish and gravy at least as appealing as meat.

Quick-fried and Braised Fish in Black Bean and Chilli Sauce (for 4-6 people to be served with rice with 1-2 other dishes)

This dish can be cooked by simply repeating the previous recipe, except the pieces of fish should be temporarily removed and put aside after the first 3-4 mins' frying and into the 'sauce' should be added 2 tsp salted black beans (which should be previously soaked in water for 10 mins) together with 1 tsp chilli sauce and 4 tbs water. The 'sauce' and ingredients should then be poured into the wok for 1½ mins' stir-frying together over high heat immediately after the pieces of fish have been removed to be put aside. The pieces of fish are then returned into the wok to be cooked in the 'sauce' for a further 4 mins (2 mins under cover) before the dish is ready for serving. Because of the stronger-tasting sauce, some find this dish even more appealing than the previous one.

Quick-fried and Braised Fish in Sweet and Sour Sauce (for 4-6 people to be eaten with rice and 1-2 other dishes)

The only difference between this dish and the previous two is that the 'sauce' is different. The sauce is concocted with the following ingredients:

    2 tbs sugar
    3 tbs vinegar
    2 tbs tomato puree
    3 tbs orange juice
    1½ tbs soya sauce
    1½ tbs cornflour (blended with 6 tbs water)

Mix these ingredients together until they are well blended. Cut one medium green pepper into 2.5 cm × 12 mm (1 in × ½ in) pieces (remove seeds).

When the pieces of fish have been removed from the wok after the first 3-5 mins' quick but static frying (turning over every minute), add the peppers into the wok. Stir them around a couple of times, pour in the sauce mixture. Stir until the sauce thickens. Immediately return the pieces of fish into the wok to cook in the sauce over gentle heat. Leave them to cook in it for 2-3 mins and the dish is ready to serve.

Soft-fried Sliced Fish in Meat-Gravy Sauce (for 4-6 people with 1-2 other dishes)

    400-600 g (1-1½ lb) filleted fish (sole, plaice, halibut, shad, bream – any fish which can be filleted and sliced thinly)
    1½ tsp salt

1 tbs cornflour
½ egg white
6 large mushrooms (or use Chinese dried mushrooms if
  available)
2 slices root-ginger
2 stalks spring onion
2½ tbs vegetable oil
1 tbs lard

Sauce
6 tbs any red-cooked meat or poultry gravy
2 tbs stock
1 tsp sugar
1 tbs soya sauce
2 tbs sherry or wine (red or white)

Preparation
Cut fish into 5 cm × 2.5 cm (2 in × 1 in) pieces. Rub with
salt, cornflour and wet with egg-white. Leave to season for
10 mins. Cut mushrooms in half after removing stalks (if
using dried mushroom soak first in water for 30 mins and
drain). Mix sauce ingredients in a bowl. Shred ginger and
cut spring onions into 12 mm (½ in) shavings.

Cooking and Serving
Heat oil and lard in the wok. When hot, add ginger and
mushroom. Stir them in the hot fat/oil for 2 mins. Add
spring onion and sauce mixture. Stir them around until the
mixture begins to boil. Add the pieces of fish into the
mixture. Stir and turn them around gently until each piece
of fish is well-covered or submerged. Leave the contents to
cook gently for 4 mins, turning over once every minute.
Serve on a well-heated dish placed in the centre of the table
for the diners to help themselves. Another great dish to be
eaten with rice.

Soft-fried Sliced Fish in Peking Wine Sauce *(for 4-6 people to be served with 1-2 savoury dishes)*

Repeat the previous recipe, preparing the fish and mushrooms in the same way, and for the 'meat-gravy sauce' substitute a wine-sauce made by blending 6 tbs good chicken stock with 4 tbs white wine or Chinese rice-wine, 1 tsp sugar and 1 tbs cornflour. The mushrooms, ginger and spring onion (reduced by half) should be put into the wok to quick-fry for 1½ mins before adding the 'sauce'. As soon as the sauce thickens, add the fish well spaced out in the wok, turning the pieces over a couple of times in the sauce and leave them to simmer together for 4-5 mins when they should be ready to serve. This is a light-coloured dish and is best eaten with rice and one or two other savoury dishes.

Dry-fried Spicy Fish *(for 4-5 or more people to be served with 1-2 other dishes)*

  400-600 g (1-1½ lb) small fish (small herrings, sardines, whiting, sprats etc.)
  2 tsp salt
  3 slices root-ginger
  5-6 tbs vegetable oil
  4-5 tbs lard

Sauce
  1 tbs salted black beans (soak in 5 tbs water for 10 mins)
  2 stalks spring onion
  2 tsp chilli sauce
  2 tbs stock
  2 tbs vinegar
  2 tbs wine (red or white)

Preparation
Clean and rub the fish with salt and chopped ginger and

leave to season for a few hours (3-4 hours or overnight). Mix the ingredients for the sauce in a bowl.

Cooking and Serving
Heat oil and lard in the wok. When hot, add the fish and see that each one of them is submerged in the hot oil/fat. Turn them around slowly for about 8-9 mins over medium heat when the fish should be quite crisp. Drain all the hot oil/fat away and sprinkle and pour the sauce mixture evenly over the fish. Turn the fish over gently to cook in the sauce. When the sauce is nearly dry transfer fish onto a heat-proof dish. Place the fish in a pre-heated oven at about 200°C (400°F) gas mark 6 for a further 6-7 mins when the fish should become even crisper. Such fish is best eaten with a copious amount of rice; its spiciness contrasts well with the blandness of the rice.

SEMI-SOUP FISH DISHES

There is another style of Chinese fish dishes, where the fish served is made to look as if it is still in its natural habitat. Because of the combined presence of fish, vegetables and clear soup with one or two dried foods, there is the appearance of the fish being still in the pond or stream with plants, twigs and different odds and ends all floating around – albeit in a hot savoury stream. This type of semi-soup dish is very welcome to rice-eaters, because it is always a pleasure to wash down a mixed mouthful of foods with a hot savoury drink.

Fish in Soup with Vegetables and Transparent Pea-Starch Noodles

    1-2 whole fish 600-800 g (1½-2 lb) trout, rainbow trout, large herring, carp, mullet etc.)
    2 tsp salt

3 slices root-ginger
2-3 stalks 'Golden Needles' (lily-bud stems)
100 g (¼ lb) transparent pea-starch noodles (available from Chinese food stores)
2-3 rashers bacon
200 g (½ lb) Brussels sprouts
3 stalks spring onion
5-6 tbs vegetable oil
750 ml (1½ pint) good stock
1 chicken stock cube
1 tsp sesame oil

Preparation

Clean fish and rub with salt and chopped and minced ginger. Leave to season for 30 mins. Cut 'needles' into 5cm (2in) segments and soak them in water with transparent noodles for 10 mins and drain. Cut bacon into matchstick shreds, and sprouts into quarters after removing discoloured leaves and tougher parts of the stem. Cut spring onions into 5 cm (2 in) segments.

Cooking and Serving

Heat oil in the wok. When hot, add bacon. Stir the strips around a couple of times and lay the fish in one piece in the hot oil in the wok. Baste the fish continually with the oil for 3 mins. Turn the fish around and baste for another 2-3 mins. Drain away any excess oil and lift the fish out to put aside. Add the sprouts into the wok. Stir-fry them in the remaining oil for 2 mins. Add half the spring onions, stock, stock cube and noodles. Bring the contents to the boil. Return the fish into the wok and submerge it under the soup and noodles. Reduce heat and leave to simmer for 12 mins. Sprinkle the top of the fish-soup and noodles with sesame oil and remaining spring onions. Serve in a deep-sides oval dish at the centre of the table for the diners to help themselves.

Fish in Soup with Bean Curd, Chinese Dried Mushrooms and Vegetables *(for 5-6 people with one or two other dishes)*

This is a similar sort of dish to the previous recipe except that bean curd is used instead of noodles and wine and dried mushrooms are added to enhance and vary the flavour.

1-2 whole fish (similar to previous recipe)
2 tsp salt
3 slices root-ginger
1 medium onion
2 rashers bacon
2 cakes bean curd
5-6 medium Chinese dried mushrooms
2 garlic cloves
2 stalks spring onion
5-6 tbs vegetable oil
750 ml (1½ pints) good stock
1 chicken stock cube
4-5 tbs white wine (or dry sherry)
1 tbs soya sauce
1 tsp sesame oil

Preparation

Clean fish and rub with salt and shredded ginger. Leave to season for 30 mins-1 hour. Cut onion into thin slices and bacon into matchstick strips, bean curd into large sugar-lump-sized pieces. Soak dried mushrooms in warm water for 30 mins, discard stalks and cut caps into quarters. Crush and chop garlic. Cut spring onions into 6 mm (¼ in) shavings.

Cooking and Serving

Heat oil in the wok. When hot, add onion and bacon. Stir them in the hot oil for 2 mins. Add the fish and turn in the oil with the other ingredients for 3-4 mins. Drain away excess oil and pour in the stock. Add stock cube, mushrooms, garlic. Bring the contents to the boil and allow them to simmer together for 10 mins. Sprinkle them with wine, soya sauce and spring onions. Simmer for a further 2-3 mins. Sprinkle with sesame oil and place in a deep-sided oval dish and serve at the centre of the table for the diners to help themselves.

Fish in Hot 'Soya Jam' Sauce *(for 4-6 people with one or two other dishes)*

600-800 g (1½-2 lb) fish (any large cut of fish: cod, halibut, haddock, bream, carp etc.)
2 tsp salt
3 slices root-ginger
1½ tbs cornflour
2-3 rashers bacon
1 medium green or red pepper
1-2 chilli peppers
4 Chinese dried mushrooms
1 tbs salted black beans
2 stalks spring onion
4 tbs vegetable oil
1 medium onion
1½ tbs lard
50-75 g (2-3 oz) minced pork
2 tbs tomato puree
1½ tbs soya sauce
1 tbs sugar
3 tbs dry sherry (or red wine)
5-6 tbs stock

Preparation
Cut fish into 5 cm × 5 cm (2 in × 2 in) rough-cut chunky pieces. Rub with salt, chopped ginger and dust with

cornflour. Leave to season for 30 mins. Cut bacon into matchstick shreds. Cut pepper into 2.5 cm (1 in) pieces. Chop chilli pepper coarsely, after discarding seeds. Soak Chinese mushrooms for 10 mins, discard stalks and cut caps into a dozen pieces. Soak black beans for 5 mins and drain. Cut spring onions into 12 mm (½ in) shavings.

Cooking and Serving

Heat oil in a wok. When hot, add onion and bacon. Stir-fry them for 2 mins. Add fish and turn the pieces gently with the other ingredients for 4 mins, remove them and put aside. Drain away any excess oil/fat. Add lard, pork, mushrooms and chilli pepper. Stir them over high heat for 3-4 mins. Add black beans, tomato puree, soya sauce and sugar. Stir and mash them together with the other ingredients for 2 mins. Pour in the wine and stock. Bring to the boil and stir them and the ingredients together. Return the pieces of fish and turn and cover them with the sauce and other ingredients in the wok. Reduce heat and leave them to cook together for 4-5 mins. Sprinkle contents with spring onion shavings. Serve by placing the pieces of fish on a well-heated serving dish and pour the sauce and ingredients in the wok over them. Because of its strong earthy spiciness this is an excellent dish to consume with a copious amount of rice.

Crustaceans

Quick-fried Giant Prawns in Shells in Hot Sauce (for 4-6 people with 1-2 other dishes)

This is a dish which is cooked in a very similar way to the fish in the previous recipe, except more shortly. The enjoyment of consuming prawns cooked in this manner is to chew and suck at the sauce on the shells before eating the prawn meat inside.

500-600 g (1¼-1½ lb) large prawns in their shell (fresh or frozen)
1½ tsp salt
2 slices root-ginger
1 medium onion
3 tsp salted black beans
4 tbs vegetable oil
50 g (2 oz) minced pork
¾ tbs soya sauce
1½ tbs tomato puree
1½ tsp sugar
1 tsp chilli sauce
3 tbs red wine
3 tbs good stock

Preparation
Brush and clean prawns under running water. Rub with salt and chopped ginger. Cut onion into thin slices and then chop coarsely. Soak black beans in water for 5 mins and drain.

Cooking and Serving
Heat oil in the wok. Add onion and stir it over high heat

for 1 min. Add the prawns and stir them in the hot oil with onion for 3 mins. Remove and put aside. Add minced pork to stir-fry in the remaining oil for 1½ mins. Add black beans and mash them with the pork against the wok for 1 min. Add soya sauce, tomato puree, sugar, chilli, wine and stock. Mix them together into a creamy sauce. When it starts to boil, return the prawns into the wok, to turn and mix with the other ingredients. When the liquid (or sauce) in the wok has reduced to less than half (in about 2½ mins) the dish is ready to serve.

Serve on a well-heated serving dish. These prawns are excellent served as a starter to complement drinks or they can be consumed with a copious amount of rice.

Quick-fried Shrimps with Peas *(for 4-5 people with 1-2 other dishes)*

500-600 g (1¼-1½ lb) shrimps (shelled, fresh or frozen)
1½ tsp salt
2 slices root-ginger
2 stalks spring onion
2 tbs lard
½ tbs vegetable oil
100-300 g (¼-¾ lb) garden peas (fresh or frozen)
½ tsp sugar
2 tbs good stock
2 tbs white wine
1½ tbs soya sauce
1 tsp sesame oil

Preparation, Cooking and Serving

Rub shrimps with salt, oil and chopped ginger (chopped coarsely). Cut spring onions into 6 mm (¼ in) shavings. Heat lard and oil in a frying-pan. When hot, add the shrimps and stir-fry quickly over high heat for 1½ mins, remove and put aside. Add spring onions and peas and stir them in the remaining oil for 1½ mins. Add sugar, stock, wine, soya sauce and bring the contents to a quick boil. Return the shrimps into the wok to mix and stir together with all the other ingredients for 1½ mins. Sprinkle with sesame oil and serve immediately on a well-heated dish. This is an excellent dish to consume on its own with sips of drink or it can be consumed with a copious amount of rice.

CRABS AND LOBSTERS

Crabs and lobsters are cooked in a very similar fashion in Chinese cooking. The following recipes can be used for either crabs or lobsters.

Cantonese Onion and Ginger Lobster or Crab *(for 4-5 people eaten as an accompaniment to drinks)*

    2 medium onions
    4 slices root-ginger
    1 medium 1.25-1.5 kg (3-4 lb) lobster (or if crab is used
        an 800 g-1 kg (2-2½ lb) crab)
    3 stalks spring onion
    6-8 tbs vegetable oil
    4 tbs minced pork
    1 tsp salt
    6 tbs good stock
    2 tbs soya sauce
    4 tbs dry sherry

Preparation
Cut onions into very thin slices and ginger into shreds. Crack the shell of the crab (if crab is used) and the main shell into two and cut the body into 6-8 pieces with a leg attached to each piece. Chop the lobster across the body

into approximately 7.5 cm (3 in) segments. Crack with the back of the chopper at 3-4 points. Cut spring onions into 5 cm (2 in) sections.

Cooking and Serving

Heat oil in the wok. When hot add the onion and ginger and the lobster segments or crab pieces. Stir and turn them over high heat for 4-5 mins. Remove the lobster (or crab) and drain away excess oil. Add pork and sprinkle with salt. Stir over high heat for 1½ mins. Pour in the stock, soya sauce and sherry. Stir them together until well mixed and the liquid is boiling. Return the lobster segments or crab pieces into the wok. Sprinkle them with spring onion. Turn the contents over half a dozen times. Place a lid over the wok and leave to cook still over high heat for 3 mins. Open the lid, turn once more and serve immediately. Much of the pleasure of eating this dish lies in sucking at the shells and extracting the meat of the lobster or crab in your mouth. Comparatively simple as the dish is, the sauce derived from the cooking is about as savoury and appealing as anything else in the whole culinary world.

A variation to the foregoing is to add an 'egg sauce' to the crab or lobster a minute or so before it is ready. This is done by beating an egg in 5-6 tbs of good stock (with ¼ tsp salt added) for 10 secs. Pour the mixture over the contents of the wok evenly immediately after opening the lid of the wok. When the egg coagulates, turn the contents over once or twice just before dishing out and serving. The 'egg sauce' provides additional material to suck at when eating the dish.

Cantonese Lobster or Crab in Black Bean Sauce (for 4-5 people to accompany drink)

Use the previous recipe. Reduce soya sauce by 1 tbs and instead add 1 tbs salted black beans (after soaking them in water for 10 mins and draining). Add them into the frying-pan when minced pork is added and mash them together against the wok just before adding the stock, sherry, soya sauce etc. 1 tsp chilli sauce may also be added to further enhance the spiciness of the flavour, but no 'egg sauce' should be added into black bean mixture as the latter already imparts a high 'earthy savouriness' to the dish and egg would make the dish too messy both in appearance and flavour-wise. For lovers of spicy food this dish is another winner.

Quick-fried Scallop with Diced Pork, Cucumber and Chicken Liver *(for 4-6 people with one or two other dishes)*

100 g (¼ lb) chicken liver
200 g (½ lb) fillet of pork
7 cm (3 in) section of medium cucumber
3-4 scallops
2 slices root-ginger
2 garlic cloves
2 tbs Chinese 'snow pickle' (or 5 cm (2 in) section medium gherkin)
1½ tsp salt
2 tbs vegetable oil
1 tbs lard
1½ tbs soya sauce
2 tbs good stock
2 tbs dry sherry

Preparation
Dice chicken liver, pork, cucumber, scallops all into 6-12 mm (¼-½ in) cubes. Chop ginger, garlic and 'snow pickle' (or gherkin) coarsely. Sprinkle scallops, liver, pork with salt and ginger and leave to season for 15 mins.

Cooking and Serving
Heat oil and lard in the wok. When hot, add garlic, pork,

and liver and stir-fry them quickly over high heat for 1 min. Add scallops and continue to stir-fry for 1½ mins. Push them to one side of the wok. Add 'pickle' and cucumber to the other side of the wok. Sprinkle them with soya sauce, stock and sherry. When contents start to boil furiously, stir and turn all the ingredients together for 2 mins. Serve on a well-heated dish to be eaten immediately.

Steaming

Steaming is a method which is used in Chinese cooking either to cook very quickly or over a good length of time. When the food is very fresh and the purpose is to bring out the freshness and natural flavour in the foods, the method employed is usually 'open steaming' which seldom lasts more than 10-15 minutes, often shorter. When the food material is somewhat tough and the purpose of cooking is to reduce the food to extreme tenderness with great richness of flavour, the method employed is usually 'closed steaming', which is a protracted form of cooking seldom lasting less than 2 hours, often much longer. Both methods are used in China with great regularity and success as in the majority of Chinese kitchens there is no oven and steaming is used in much the same way as baking is used in the western kitchen (hence in China the bread and buns are steamed rather than baked and are white and soft-skinned rather than brown and crusty).

In steaming with a wok you will need a round Chinese 'basket-steamer' (or any round large cake-tin-shaped utensil with a wire-mesh bottom and firm lid to close it on top) which will sit 2.5-4 cm (1-1½ in) inside the wok which is half-filled with boiling water. If the water is kept at a rolling boil, a continuous volume of steam will rise or gush through the steamer or steamers (often several 'basket-steamers' can be placed and fitted one on top of the other). To be effective, one has to be sure that the wok is a reasonably large one and that there is a sufficient quantity of boiling water in the wok to generate the necessary volume of steam to cook effectively, even in a short time. Since the 'steamer' is sitting inside the wok, the water in the wok can be replenished simply by pouring additional boiling water into the wok down the sides.

'West Lake' Steamed Fish *(for 4-6 people with other dishes)*

This is a simple but famous dish, said to be derived from the West Lake of Hangchow.

    1 800 g-1.25 kg (2-3 lb) whole fish (bream, carp trout, salmon, mullet etc)
    1½ tsp salt
    2½ tbs soya sauce
    2 tbs vinegar
    1½ tsp sugar
    2 tbs chopped 'snow pickles' (or gherkins)
    4 slices large root-ginger
    6 stalks spring onion
    2 tbs lard (or butter)

Preparation

Clean and rub fish – both inside and out – with salt, soya sauce, vinegar, sugar and chopped pickles. Leave to season for 30 mins-1 hour (turning the fish over a couple of times). Cut ginger into shreds and spring onions into 7.5 cm (3 in) sections.

Cooking and Serving

Place the fish on an oval dish. Dress it from head to tail with shreds of ginger and spring onion and pour the remainder of the 'marinade' over its length. Place the dish in the steamer (it will have to be a very large one) and steam vigorously for 20 mins. Heat lard or butter in a small pan. When it froths, pour it over the length of the fish and serve by bringing the oval dish containing the whole fish to the table. The flesh of the fish should be easily picked from the bones and should be eaten after dipping in the sauce which has accumulated in the oval dish during the steaming.

Steamed Short-Cut Pork and Black Bean Spare-ribs *(for 4-5 people with 1-2 other dishes)*

600-800 g (1½-2 lb) pork spare-ribs
2 slices root-ginger (chopped coarsely)
1½ tbs salted black beans
1½ tsp salt
pepper (to taste)
1½ tbs chopped parsley
1 tbs cornflour
1½ tbs vegetable oil

Preparation

Chop spare-ribs through bones into 2.5 cm (1 in) sections. Shred ginger. Soak black beans in water for 20 mins and drain. Rub the spare-ribs with salt, ginger, black beans, pepper, parsley, cornflour and oil. Rub and mix them up thoroughly. Leave them to season for 1 hour (or longer).

Cooking and Serving

Place the spare-ribs on a round heat-proof dish and insert it into a 'steamer' which is pre-heated on top of the wok in which the water is kept at a rolling boil. Steam the ribs vigorously for 12-15 mins and serve by bringing the dish directly to the table.

This is a 'starter' for the diners to nibble at as they sip their drinks.

Steamed Spring Chicken with Black Beans and Young Leeks *(for 4-6 people with 1–2 other dishes)*

800 g-1.25 kg (2-3 lb) spring chicken
1 tbs salted black beans
3 slices root-ginger
2 garlic cloves

1½ tsp salt
pepper (to taste)
2 tbs vegetable oil
3-4 stalks young leeks
2 tbs dry sherry

Preparation

Chop chicken through bone into 20-25 bite-sized pieces. Soak black beans in water for 10 mins and drain. Cut ginger into shreds, crush garlic and chop coarsely. Rub the ginger, black beans, salt, pepper and oil into the chicken pieces. Leave to season for 1 hour. Clean and cut the leeks diagonally into 4 cm (1½ in) sections. Pack the chicken pieces into a heat-proof basin or deep-sided dish, interleaving them with the leeks. Pour sherry evenly over the contents.

Cooking and Serving

Place the basin or dish in the basket-steamer. Turn the heat high to generate the maximum volume of steam. Steam vigorously for 30 mins. Serve by bringing the basin or deep-sided dish to the table. A good dish to serve along with one or two stir-fried dishes.

Steamed Cabbage-wrapped Beef *(for 4-6 people with 1-2 other dishes)*

2 slices root-ginger
2 stalks spring onion
300 g (¾ lb) minced beef
1½ tsp salt
pepper (to taste)
¾ tsp sugar
1 tbs soya sauce
1 tbs cornflour
½ egg
100 g (¼ lb) minced pork
12 medium-sized cabbage leaves

For Sauce
  1½ tbs soya sauce
  ¾ tbs wine vinegar
  1½ tsp sesame oil

Preparation
Chop ginger coarsely. Cut spring onions into fine shavings. Mix them with the beef together with salt, pepper, sugar, soya sauce, cornflour, beaten egg and minced pork. Knead and mix them well until all the ingredients are well mixed. Divide the mixture into 12 portions.

Dip the cabbage leaves in boiling water for 1½ mins to soften. Wrap each portion of minced meat in a cabbage leaf. Mix sauce ingredients together in a bowl.

Cooking and Serving
Place the cabbage-wrapped 'packages' on a heat-proof dish. Insert the dish in a steamer and steam vigorously for 25 mins. Serve by sprinkling with sauce mixture and bringing the dish to the table. Another good dish to serve with stir-fried dishes.

Steamed Minced Pork with Cauliflower *(for 4-6 people with 1-2 other dishes)*

  1 small onion
  1 egg
  400 g (1 lb) minced pork
  1 tbs chopped gherkin (or pickles)
  1 tsp sugar
  2 tbs soya sauce (or 1½ tbs soya sauce with ¾ tbs soya paste)
  1 tbs cornflour
  1 tbs dry sherry
  1 small cauliflower
  1 tsp salt

Preparation

Cut onion into thin slices and chop coarsely. Beat egg lightly with a fork for 10 secs. Add the onion and beaten egg to the pork along with gherkin (or pickles), sugar, soya sauce, cornflour, sherry and beaten egg. Knead or mix with a wooden spoon until all the ingredients are evenly mixed. Break cauliflower into 4-5 cm (1½-2 in) flowerets. Place them at the bottom of heat-proof basin. Sprinkle with salt and pack the pork mixture on top of the cauliflower. Pack evenly so that all the vegetables are well covered.

Cooking and Serving

Place the basin in the steamer over the wok and steam vigorously for 45 mins. Or, alternatively, if a steamer is not available the basin could be simply placed in the wok surrounded by 7.5-9 cm (3-3½ in) of boiling water and a lid placed over the wok. The contents will steam effectively if the water is kept at a rolling boil for 35 mins (be sure to keep the water well-replenished by pouring in boiling water from a kettle). Serve by bringing the basin directly to the table. A conventional dish often served with stir-fried dishes during a Chinese family dinner.

Steamed Sliced Pork with Sliced Yam *(for 4-6 people with 1-2 other dishes)*

600 g (1½ lb) lean and fat pork
1-1.25 kg (2½-3 lb) yam (or sweet potato)
3 tbs soya sauce
1 tbs red bean-curd 'cheese' (optional)
1 tsp sugar
2 tbs good stock
300-400 g (¾-1 lb) broccoli
3½ tbs vegetable oil

Preparation
Cut pork into 7.5 cm × 4 cm × 4 mm (3 in × 1½ in × ⅙ in)
oblong slices. Cut yam as near as possible into similarly
sized pieces but double the pork's thickness. Mix soya
sauce with bean-curd 'cheese', sugar and stock in a bowl.
Break broccoli tops into individual flowerets.

Cooking and Serving
Heat oil in a large frying-pan. Add pork and the mixed
sauce in bowl. Turn them over high heat for 3-4 mins until
all the pieces of pork are well-covered with the sauce.
Remove from heat and sandwich each piece of pork in
between 2 slices of yam. Hold about 6 'sandwiches'
together with a toothpick or wooden or bamboo skewer.
Return the frying-pan over the heat. Add all the broccoli
tops to stir around in the remaining oil and sauce for 1
min.

Arrange the broccoli around the heat-proof dish and
place the skewered pork and yam sandwiches in the centre.
Insert the dish in the steamer over the wok to steam
vigorously for 20 mins and serve by bringing the dish to the
table after removing skewers. A pretty and, at the same
time, curiously satisfying dish (partly because most of the
fatness of the pork has been absorbed by the sandwiches of
yam).

LONG-COOKED CLOSE-STEAMED DISHES

All dishes of this category are steamed in a pot or
receptacle which is closed. This is done by placing the food
to be cooked in a casserole with a lid which can be firmly
closed during the whole period of cooking, or the top of
the containing receptacle is firmly closed by the use of a
sheet of tin foil or greaseproof paper which ties firmly
around the top of the pot or basin.

Aromatic Steamed Pork with Ground Rice *(for 4-6 people with 1-2 other dishes)*

800 g (2 lb) belly of pork
3 tbs soya sauce
2 tsp red bean-curd 'cheese' (optional)
1½ tbs dry sherry
5-6 tbs coarsely ground rice

Preparation
Cut pork through skin into 5 cm × 4 cm × 1½ cm (2 in × 1½ in × 1 in) pieces, each piece with skin attached. Sprinkle and rub thoroughly with soya sauce, soya bean-curd 'cheese' and sherry. Leave to season for 30 mins. Meanwhile grind rice coarsely in a mortar. Heat the rice in a dry frying-pan over low heat, stirring now and then until brown and aromatic. Apply this aromatic ground rice to the pieces of pork until each piece is well covered.

Cooking and Serving
Pack the ground rice-covered pork into a heat-proof dish. Cover the top of the basin firmly with a sheet of tin foil. Place the basin in 9 cm (3½ in) of water, standing firmly in the centre of the wok. Bring water to the boil and place a lid over the wok. Keep the water in the wok at a simmer for 3½-4 hours.

Serve by bringing the basin containing the pork to the table. After the long cooking the pieces of pork should be very tender and aromatic and what there is of fat should be absorbed by the ground rice. This is one of the favourite dishes of the people in China.

Long-Cooked Pork Tripe and Belly of Pork *(for 4-6 people with 1-2 other dishes)*

400 g (1 lb) tripe
2 tsp salt

400 g (1 lb) belly of pork
2 medium onions
3 tbs soya sauce
1½ tbs dry sherry
½ chicken stock cube
4 tbs good stock
2 stalks spring onion

Preparation
Rub tripe with salt and leave to season for 1 hour. Rinse
quickly and pat dry. Cut tripe into 6.5 cm × 2.5 cm (2½
× 1 in) strips. Cut pork through skin into 5 cm × 4 cm ×
2.5 cm (2 in × 1½ in × 1 in) pieces. Cut onions into thin
slices. Place pork, tripe, and onion in a basin. Add soya
sauce, sherry and crumbled chicken stock cube, sprinkle
with stock and chopped spring onion. Mix them well
together. Pack the tripe, onion and pork into a heat-proof
dish, interleaving them as evenly as possible.

Cooking and Serving
Close the top of the pot (with a sheet of tin foil) or if a
casserole is used, close the lid of the casserole. Place the
casserole or pot in the wok to stand in 7.5-9 cm (3-3½ in)
of boiling water. Cover the top of the wok and leave the
water to simmer gently for 4 hours. Serve by bringing the
pot or casserole to the table. Pork and trip so cooked are
extremely succulent and excellent to eat with a copious
amount of rice and one pure vegetable dish.

Long-Steamed Knuckles of Pork *(for 6-8 people with 1-2
other dishes)*

Knuckles of pork are still extremely cheap in the English-
speaking world. Use 2 of them (each weighing about
800 g-1.25 kg (2-3 lb) with the bone). Add a pair of pig's

trotters which can sometimes be obtained free from the butcher.

2 knuckles of pork
2 pork trotters
5 tbs soya sauce
250 ml (½ pint) good stock
250 ml (½ pint) red wine
1 tbs sugar

Preparation and Cooking
Scrub the knuckles and trotters clean under running water, pat dry. Place them at the bottom of a casserole. Pour in the soya sauce, stock, wine and sugar. Turn the meat around a few times in the 'marinade', close the lid of the casserole and place it in the centre of the wok to stand in 7.5-9 cm (3-3½ in) boiling water. Place a cover over the wok and keep the water in it at a simmer for the next 4 hours, turning the contents in the casserole around every hour.

Serving
Bring the casserole directly to the table. Apart from the meat and skin, which should now be extremely tender (the skin should be treated as jelly) there should be ample gravy. Because of the quantity of the bone and skin which are long-cooked together, the gravy will have a special 'sticky' quality. When applied to plain boiled rice and some lightly-cooked green vegetables, one touches one of the high points of the whole Chinese cuisine in savoury succulence.

Long-Steamed Brisket of Beef *(for 4-6 people with 1-2 other dishes)*

600-800 g (1½-2 lb) brisket of beef
1 tsp salt

pepper (to taste)
1 large onion
2 sprigs of parsely
3 tbs vegetable oil
3-4 slices root-ginger
3 tbs soya sauce
250 ml (½ pint) water (or stock)

Preparation
Cut the beef with a sharp knife into 4 cm (1½ in) cubes.
Sprinkle and rub with salt and pepper. Cut onion into
slices. Chop parsley coarsely.

Cooking and Serving
Heat oil in a large frying-pan. Add ginger, onion and beef.
Stir-fry over high heat for 4-5 mins. Transfer contents into
a small casserole. Add the soya sauce and water and bring
to the boil. Place the casserole in the centre of the wok to
stand in 9 cm (3½ in) of boiling water. Keep water at a
simmer for 3½-4 hours replenishing the water in the wok
when necessary, turning the beef over once every hour.
Sprinkle the top of the beef with chopped parsely and
bring the casserole directly to the table for the diners to
help themselves. The beef should now be very tender and
the gravy ample. A great dish for rice-eaters. Beef so
cooked can also be eaten with plain boiled noodles.

Long-Cooked Steamed Ginger Mutton or Lamb *(for 4-6 people with 1-2 other dishes)*

600-800 g (1½-2 lb) lamb (or mutton)
200 g (½ lb) turnips
1½ tsp salt
pepper (to taste)
2½ tbs vegetable oil
6 slices root-ginger

3 tbs soya sauce
250 ml (½ pint) white sauce
125 ml (¼ pint) water (or stock)

Preparation
Cut lamb (or mutton) into 4 cm (1½ in) cubes and turnips diagonally into 4 cm (1½ in) wedge-shaped pieces. Rub meat with salt and pepper.

Cooking and Serving
Heat oil in a small casserole. When hot, add ginger and lamb. Stir and turn them over medium heat for 5-6 mins. Add all the other ingredients and bring to the boil. Place the casserole in the centre of the wok to stand in 9 cm (3½ in) of boiling water. Keep the water at a simmer for the next 3½-4 hours, turning the contents over every hour. Serve in the casserole for the diners to help themselves.

Long-Steamed Soya Chicken or Duck with Chestnuts
(for 6-8 people with 1-2 other dishes)

1 1.25-1.5 kg (3-4 lb) chicken or duck
400 g (1 lb) chestnuts
3 slices root-ginger
3 tbs vegetable oil
5 tbs soya sauce
4 tbs stock
4 tbs red wine

Preparation
Chop bird through bones into 25-30 large bite-size pieces. Shell the chestnuts after blanching for 2 mins in boiling water. Shred the ginger.

Cooking and Serving
Heat oil in a large frying-pan. When hot, add the chicken or duck pieces and ginger and turn them over high heat for

4-5 mins. Transfer them into a casserole. Add chestnuts, soya sauce, stock and wine. Bring them to the boil on top of the cooker, turning the solids over in the sauce a few times. Place the casserole in the centre of a large wok to stand in 9 cm (3½ in) of boiling water. Keep the water at a simmer for the next 3½ hours, turning the contents over every hour. Serve by bringing the casserole to the table. The meat of the birds should be tender enough to be easily detached in the mouth from the bones. The enjoyment of consuming this dish with rice lies not only in eating the meats but in the jelly-like melting quality of the skin and tendons.

Long-Steamed Multi-layer 'Meat Pudding' (for 4-6 people with 1-2 other dishes)

    600 g (1½ lb) belly of pork
    400 g (1 lb) yam (or potato)
    100 g (¼ lb) carrots
    4 tbs chopped Chinese salted 'snow pickles' (or a 7.5 cm
        (3 in) piece of medium gherkin)
    1 orange
    4 tbs vegetable oil
    100 g (¼ lb) minced pork
    1 tsp salt
    3 tbs soya sauce
    2 tbs red wine

Preparation
Cut pork and yam into 4 cm (1½ in) pieces and carrots diagonally into pieces half the size. Chop pickle or gherkin coarsely and orange into a dozen wedges.

Cooking and Serving
Heat half the oil in a frying-pan. Add minced pork, salt and half the chopped pickles. Stir-fry them together and

place and pack them into the bottom of a deep heat-proof basin or pot. Place the yam pieces on top. Heat the balance of oil in the frying-pan. When hot, add the pork to stir-fry in it over medium heat for 2 mins. Sprinkle with soya sauce and continue to stir-fry for 2 mins. Place half the pork over the yam. Spread the orange pieces over the first layer of pork and place the remainder of the pork as a second layer on top of the orange. Sprinkle the remainder of the pickle, the remainder of the soya sauce in the frying-pan and the wine over the contents.

Place the basin or pot in the centre of the wok to stand in 9 cm (3½ in) of boiling water. Close the top of the wok with a lid and keep the water to boil at a simmer for the next 3½ hours. Bring the pot or basin to the table and serve. By this time, both the yam and carrots will have absorbed a great deal of the savouriness of the meat and they will also have absorbed a good proportion of their richness. A very satisfying dish for those who are hungry.

Egg Dishes

Eggs are either quick-fried or shortly steamed. When steamed, they are usually beaten and blended with stock and served as a kind of savoury, junkety custard which is very satisfying to consume with rice. When quick-fried or stir-fried, some small amount of 'yellow wine' (similar to sherry) is usually added at the last moment along with chopped chives or spring onions which give the dish a very appetizing aromatic fragrance. Whichever way it is done, eggs make for simple dishes which can be knocked up, cooked and served in a very little time, although timing in cooking is important (in Chinese quick-fried or stir-fried egg dishes the eggs are not allowed to set as firmly or solidly as in a Spanish omelette). Usually in the cooking the eggs should be given a stir in the wok when it is 75 per cent set and served immediately after sprinkling it with the aromatic ingredients (chopped chives and sherry).

Quick-fried Eggs with Shrimps *(for 3-4 people with 1-2 other dishes)*

4-5 eggs
1 tsp salt
4-5 tbs shrimps (fresh, frozen or cooked)
2½ tbs vegetable oil
1 tbs lard (or butter)
1½ tbs chopped spring onion or chives (coarsely chopped)
1 tbs dry sherry
1 tbs soya sauce

Preparation

Beat eggs and salt for 10-12 seconds with a fork. Shell the shrimps (thaw first if frozen).

Cooking and Serving

Heat oil and lard in the wok. When hot, tilt the wok so that the hot oil will cover the surface of the pan. Reduce the heat to medium. Add shrimps and spread over the surface of the pan. Add eggs and after 1 min tilt the wok so that the beaten egg will cover a wider area in the wok. After a further minute, stir the eggs a couple of times, sprinkle the top of the eggs with chopped spring onion; then sprinkle evenly with sherry. Transfer the egg (now about 95-98 per cent set) to a well-heated dish. Sprinkle contents with soya sauce and serve.

Stir-fried Eggs with Bacon and Vegetables *(for 3-4 people with 1-2 other dishes)*

    4-5 eggs
    1 tsp salt
    1 small onion
    3 rashers bacon
    1 stick celery
    2 stalks spring onion
    ½ small bundle watercress
    1 small red pepper
    2½ tbs vegetable oil
    4-5 medium mushrooms
    3 tbs green peas
    1 tbs soya sauce
    1½ tbs lard (or butter)

Preparation

Beat eggs with salt for 10-12 seconds. Cut onion into very thin slices and bacon into matchstick shreds. Cut celery and spring onions into 12 mm (½ in) sections and water-cress into 2.4 cm (1 in) slices and red pepper into 12 mm (½ in) pieces (after removing seeds).

Cooking and Serving
Heat oil in the wok. When hot, add onion and bacon. Stir-fry for 1 min over high heat. Add celery, pepper and mushrooms. Stir-fry them together for 1½ mins. Add peas and watercress. Sprinkle with soya sauce and stir-fry them altogether for 1 min. Remove them from the wok to put aside. Add lard into the wok. When it has all melted, swill it around in the wok and pour in the beaten eggs. Cook over medium heat for about 2 mins when the eggs should be 90 per cent set. Stir around a couple of times. Return the cooked vegetables into the wok. Turn and stir them around with the egg for 1½ mins and serve on a well-heated dish for the diners to help themselves. A satisfying dish to consume with rice, particularly when comple-mented with a long-cooked meat dish.

Boatman's Multi-layer Seafood Omelette (for 4-5 people with 1-2 other dishes)

6 eggs
1 tsp salt
2 rashers bacon
1 medium onion
2 stalks spring onion
3 tbs oysters (or mussels)
3 garlic cloves
4½ tbs vegetable oil
3 tbs lard
2-3 tbs crab meat
1-2 tbs clam meat
3 tbs shrimps (fresh or frozen)
1½ tbs soya sauce
2 tbs green peas

Preparation
Beat eggs with salt for 10-12 seconds. Cut bacon into
matchstick shreds, onion into thin slices and spring onions
into 12 mm (½ in) shavings. Remove oysters or mussels
from shells after blanching in boiling water for 2 mins.
Crush and chop garlic coarsely.

Cooking and Serving
Heat 1½ tbs oil and ½ tbs lard in the wok. Add onion and
bacon. Stir-fry them over high heat for 1½ mins. Reduce
heat to medium and pour in ⅓ of the egg. Tilt the wok and
swill the beaten egg around and leave it to cook for 1½
mins or until set. Lift the omelette in one piece and place it
on a large well-heated serving dish.

Add 1½ tbs oil and ½ tbs lard into the wok. Add half
the garlic, crab meat, clams and spring onions into the
wok. Stir them around for 30 secs and pour in half of
the remaining egg. Tilt the wok and swill the egg around a
couple of times and leave it to cook for about 1½ mins (or
until set). Lift the omelette in one piece and lay on top of
the first omelette in the serving dish.

Add the remaining oil and lard into the wok, together
with the green peas and the remaining garlic and spring
onion. Stir them around a couple of times over medium
heat. Add the shrimps and oyster and stir together for 30
secs. Pour in the remainder of the beaten egg. Swill it
around a couple of times and allow it to cook until set. Lift
the omelette in one piece with the aid of a fish slice and
place it on top of the first two omelettes in the dish. Use a
knife to cut the 3-layer omelette through like a round cake
into eight segments. Sprinkle with soya sauce and serve.
This is an extremely tasty omelette which can be served as a
party meal.

Yellow Flowing Egg *(a Peking dish, especially created to eat with rice – for 4-6 people with 1-2 other dishes)*

3 eggs
2 egg yolks
1 tsp salt
½ chicken stock cube
6 tbs good stock
1 tbs cornflour (blended in 5 tbs water)
1½ tbs lard (or butter)
3½ tbs vegetable oil
1 tbs chopped spring onion
2-3 tbs chopped ham

Preparation
Beat eggs and yolks for 12 seconds with salt. Dissolve stock cube in the stock and blend it with cornflour mixture (already blended in water) until consistent. Pour the mixture into the beaten egg and mix well until very well blended. Melt the lard (or butter).

Cooking and Serving
Heat oil in the wok. When hot, reduce heat to low/medium. Pour in the beaten egg with stock etc. Stir gently and continually in one direction for 4 mins. Add the lard slowly and spring onion. Continue to stir for 1½ more mins. Pour the mixture into a bowl or basin. Sprinkle with chopped ham and serve. A favourite dish in Peking to consume with a copious amount of rice.

Steamed Savoury Egg Custard *(for 4-6 people with 1-2 other dishes)*

1 chicken stock cube
500 ml (1 pint) good stock
2 eggs
1 tsp salt

4 tbs chopped ham (minced)
1½ tbs chopped spring onion
1 tbs soya sauce

Preparation
Dissolve stock cube in stock. Beat egg and salt with fork for 12 secs. Add half minced ham to beaten egg and stock. Mix them together until well blended. Pour the mixture into heat-proof basin or deep-sided dish.

Cooking and Serving
Place the bowl or deep-sided dish on top of a rack or cake tin in 9 cm (3½ in) of boiling water in the wok. Place the lid over the wok and keep the water in it at a steady boil for 18 mins. Open the lid and sprinkle the top of the custard which should now be firm with the chopped spring onion and remainder of the chopped ham. Replace the lid and steam for a further 2 mins. Lift the bowl (or dish) out of the wok, sprinkle the top of the custard with soya sauce and bring it to the table. Spoons should be provided for the diners to transfer spoonfuls of the 'savoury custard' on top of their bowls of rice – to be consumed with mouthfuls of foods from other dishes on the table. 'Savoury custard' cooked in this manner is very light and excellent with any stir-fried meat or vegetable dish with plain or fried rice. It is a dish which is served frequently in Chinese homes.

Western Dishes Cooked in the Wok in the Chinese Way

As previously mentioned, the wok is essentially a round-bottomed frying-pan which can be used for braising, quick-frying, shallow-frying, deep-frying and short and long steaming (or as a double-boiler). When cooking western dishes the Chinese way one essential flavouring ingredient which can be brought into play to advantage is soya sauce (as well as the other derivatives of salted and fermented soya beans). The other Chinese ingredients which can be used to good effect are root-ginger and sesame oil. The former helps to reduce the fishiness of fish and seafoods and the other helps to improve the aromatic quality of many dishes. A small amount of sugar is regularly added in Chinese stews and braised dishes. The same could be added to a western stew to improve its richness and freshness. The final 'glossing' of vegetable or fish (if steamed) with hot lard or melted butter is a Chinese practice which can assist in making these dishes more succulent and flavoursome (the Chinese have a greater awareness of the importance of the use of flavoured oil). Chinese chefs are no respecters of conventions. They would improvise as they go along, adding Chinese touches as they think fit!

Kedgeree (for 4-5 people)

3-4 rashers of bacon
1 onion
200 g (½ lb) cooked fish (cod)
100 g (¼ lb) smoked fish (haddock)
2 stalks spring onion

2 hard-boiled eggs
1½ tbs oil
1½ tbs butter
400-500 g (1-1¾ lb) cooked rice
salt and pepper (to taste)
3-4 tbs milk
2 tsp chopped parsley (optional)

Preparation
Cut bacon into shreds and onion into thin slices. Flake the
fish, removing all bones. Clean and cut spring onion into
fine shavings. Cut and chop 1 hard-boiled egg and the
white of the other into small pieces (keep the other yolk
separate).

Cooking and Serving
Heat oil and butter in the wok. Add onion and bacon. Turn
them for 1 min in hot fat. Add both types of fish. Turn
them a few times and break them into small pieces. Add
the rice and sprinkle with salt and pepper, spring onions
and chopped eggs. Turn them together with the fish over
medium heat until evenly mixed and well heated through.
Add milk to prevent burning. Turn a few more times and
serve.

Serve by piling contents from the wok on a large well-
heated dish in a pyramid shape. Sieve the egg yolk over the
pinnacle of the pyramid, sprinkle with parsley and serve.

'Grilled' or Dry-fried Sausages with Kidney and Liver
*(foods which are shallow-fried or stir-fried in the wok have
much the same quality as if they have been grilled – for 3
people)*

3 lamb's kidneys
200-300 g (½-¾ lb) liver
1½ tbs cornflour

6 tbs vegetable oil
2 medium onions
6 sausages (pork or beef)
1 tsp sugar
½ tsp salt
1 tbs soya sauce

Preparation

Remove the membrane and gristle from the kidneys. Cut each in half. Cut liver into 3 pieces. Dust the kidney and liver pieces with cornflour and rub with 1 tbs oil. Cut onions into thin slices.

Cooking and Serving

Heat remaining oil in the wok. When hot, add the sausages. Turn each one of them in the hot fat and push it to the side. Do the same with the liver and kidney. Drain away any excess fat. Add the onions to the centre of the wok. Turn them in the remaining fat.

Reduce heat to low. Leave the different ingredients to cook slowly for the next 4-5 mins, turning them over 2-3 times in the process. Remove the kidney first into the serving dishes and then the liver. At this point, sprinkle the onion with sugar, salt and soya sauce. Turn them over a few times and leave to cook a further minute. Remove them with a perforated spoon to join the kidney and liver in the serving dishes. Excellent to eat with mashed or sauteed potatoes.

Dry-fried Mixed Grill (for 3 people)

Use the previous recipe, adding a small piece of beefsteak for each person and a smaller piece of gammon. Add the beef last with the kidney (and the sausages first) as they require the least cooking. Any excess oil or fat should be drained away after the initial frying of 2-3 mins – hence 'dry-frying' which is so frequently practised in Chinese cooking. The addition of onion, flavoured with soya sauce and sugar, should give a fresh dimension to this dish.

Braised Celery *(or any semi-hard vegetable: asparagus, courgettes, aubergines, marrows etc.)* **with Minced Meat** *(for 4 people, as a main dish or subsidiary dish)*

400-500 g (1-1¼ lb) celery
1-2 slices root-ginger
2 tbs vegetable oil
1 tbs butter
100 g (¼ lb) minced pork (or beef)
½ tsp salt
2 tbs soya sauce
3 tbs good stock
½ chicken stock cube (crumbled)
½ tsp sugar
3 tbs red wine

Preparation
Clean celery and cut diagonally into 7-5 10 cm (3-4 in) sections. Shred and mince ginger.

Cooking and Serving
Heat oil and butter in the wok. Add minced meat, sprinkle with salt and minced ginger. Stir and turn them over high heat for 2 mins. Pour in the soya sauce. Mix and turn it with the meat for 30 secs. Add the celery. Turn and mix them together with the minced meat etc. Add the stock. Sprinkle the contents with stock cube, sugar and wine. Turn a few more times. Reduce heat to low. Place a cover over the wok and leave to cook gently for 6-7 mins. If the dish is meant to be a main course – for 3 people – the minced meat content will have to be increased to 300-400 g (¾-1 lb) and the vegetables by 50 per cent. It can then be served with boiled or mashed potatoes or boiled rice for a complete meal.

Shallow-fried Fish with Onions and Vegetables *(for 3 people)*

600 g (1½ lb) fish (cod, haddock, hake etc.)
½ egg (beaten)
½ tsp salt
2 tbs cornflour
2-3 slices root-ginger
2 medium onions
1 medium red or green pepper
3 stalks spring onion
6-8 tbs vegetable oil
2 tbs soya sauce
2 tbs stock
2 tbs red wine
1 tsp sugar

Preparation

Cut fish roughly into 5 cm × 2.5 cm (2 in × 1 in) pieces. Wet with beaten egg and dust with seasoned cornflour (blend salt with cornflour). Shred ginger and cut onions and pepper into thin slices. Cut spring onions into 5 cm (2 in) sections.

Cooking and Serving

Heat oil in the wok. Lower fish piece by piece into the well of the wok. Turn them in the hot oil a couple of times and push them to the sides. When all the pieces have been initially fried, leave them to cook over medium heat for 1½ mins. Drain away all excess oil. Sprinkle fish with 1 tbs of the soya sauce. Turn them in the sauce once and lift them out to put aside.

Add the onion and pepper to the wok. Turn the heat high and stir-fry the vegetables in the remaining oil for 1 min. Pour in the remaining soya sauce, stock and wine. Sprinkle them with sugar. Turn them together a few times.

Reduce heat to low. Place the pieces of fish on top of the vegetables. Sprinkle contents with sections of spring onion. Place a cover over the wok. Leave contents to cook gently for 3-4 mins.

Ladle the vegetables and fish onto individual serving dishes. Excellent with boiled potatoes or rice.

'Hamburgers' served with Rice or Noodles (in the Chinese style for 4 people)

    3 waterchestnuts
    2½ medium onions
    2 slices root-ginger
    400 g (1 lb) minced beef
    1½ tsp salt
    1 tbs lard
    2 tbs cornflour
    1 egg
    2 tbs soya sauce
    125 ml (¼ pint) vegetable oil (to be reused)
    3 tbs good stock

Preparation
Cut and chop water-chestnuts and ½ onion coarsely. Chop ginger finely. Mix them in a basin with beef, salt, lard, 1 tbs cornflour, egg and 1 tbs soya sauce until very well mixed. Form them into 6 equal hamburgers. Dust the surface with remaining cornflour. Cut the other 2 onions into thin slices.

Cooking and Serving
Heat oil in the wok. When hot, add the 'hamburgers' one by one. Turn them in the boiling oil for about 6-7 mins (approximately 3 mins on either side). Drain away most of the oil and transfer the 'hamburgers' onto a roasting pan and insert them into a pre-heated oven at 150°C (300° F) gas mark 2 to keep hot. Add the remaining onion slices

into the remaining oil in the wok. Stir-fry them over high heat for 1½ mins. Add stock and remaining soya sauce. Stir them with the onions for 30 secs. Return the 'hamburgers' into the pan to turn together with the onion and sauce for 1 min. Divide and serve in the conventional manner with mashed potato or one of the Chinese noodle or rice dishes: Fried Rice (see page 26) or Chow Mein (see page 82

Pork Chops with Onion (Chinese style for 4 people)

Use 4 large pork chops. Rub with 2 tsp salt and pepper (to taste) and 1 tbs oil. Use the previous recipe, but fry the chops for 2 mins longer (8-9 mins) during the initial frying and add all the onions after draining away the oil (ginger and water-chestnuts can be eliminated, replacing them with 2 garlic cloves which should be added into the stir-frying when the onions are added). Best eaten with mashed potatoes or plain boiled rice or noodles, or with Chow Mein (see page 82) or Fried Rice (see page 26).

Cock-a-Leekie (for 6-8 people)

600-800 g (1½-2 lb) stewing beef
300 g (¾ lb) prunes
300 g (¾ lb) leeks (3-4 stalks)
1 medium boiling fowl
4 slices root-ginger
3 tsp salt
1 chicken stock cube
3 tbs soya sauce
1 ½ tbs sesame oil

Preparation

Cut beef into 4 cm (1½ in) pieces and fowl into joints (cut each joint again into halves). Soak prunes overnight, and clean and cut half the leeks diagonally into 4 cm (1½ in) slices.

Cooking

Heat 500 ml (2 pints) water in the wok. When it boils, add
fowl, ginger and beef. Bring to boil and then simmer for 30
mins. Skim away impurities and discard ginger. Transfer
beef and chicken into a heat-proof pan. Add salt and
remaining whole leeks. Pour in sufficient soup to cover the
solids. Place the pan in 9-10 cm (3½-4 in) water in the
centre of the work. Cover the wok and bring water to boil.
Reduce heat and cook gently at a simmer for 2½ hours.
Remove the stalks of leeks. Add prunes and carry on
simmering for 15 mins. Add the sliced leeks and stock
cube. Simmer for a further 15 mins.

Serving

Serve by dividing the beef and chicken into as many
serving dishes as there are diners. Sprinkle each dish with a
proportion of the soya sauce blended in sesame oil. Divide
the soup, leeks and prunes into as many soup-bowls.
Consume the beef and chicken and meat – a few tbs of
boiled rice or Fried Rice may be added into the meat dish –
so that they can all be eaten together as we do in China.

Minute Beefsteak with Peas, Onions and Rice *(for 2-3 people)*

   600-800 g (1½-2 lb) beefsteak (in 2-3 large thin slices)
   2½ tbs soya sauce
   ½ tsp sugar
   pepper to taste
   1½ tbs dry sherry
   2 medium onions
   3 tbs vegetable oil
   1½ tbs butter
   4-5 tbs green peas (fresh or frozen)
   300 g (¾ lb) cooked rice

Preparation

Cut each piece of steak into 3 smaller pieces. Add soya

sauce, sugar, pepper and sherry. Mix and rub them into the steak and leave to marinate for 30 mins. Drain meat and keep the marinade. Cut onions into thin slices.

Cooking

Heat oil and butter in the wok. When hot, add the onions, turn them a couple of times in the hot oil/fat and push them to one side. Add the steaks. Turn them 3-4 times in the hot oil/fat. Press them against the wok. Leave them to fry for 4 mins (2 mins on either side) covered with the onion.

Divide and transfer the steaks into a well-heated serving dish. Add peas to the wok. Turn them around a few times with the onion. Add the remainder of the marinade into the wok. Stir-fry it with the peas and onion for 1 min. Add the cooked rice. Turn it with the onion and peas (one to add flavour and the other colour). Once the rice has heated through (in about 1½ mins) divide and serve it with the steak in the serving dishes. A part Chinese and part western dish which is, however, very satisfying to consume.

Irish Stew (for 4-6 people)

1-1.25 kg (2½-3 lb) mutton (fore quarters)
800 g-1 kg (2-2½ lb) potatoes
2 large onions
4 slices root-ginger
10 peppercorns
1 chicken stock cube
2 stalks spring onion
2 medium carrots
3 tsp salt
750 ml (1½ pints) water

Preparation

Cut mutton (or lamb) into thick slices. Peel and cut potatoes into 12-18 mm (½-¾ in) slices and then cut each slice in half. Cut onions into thick slices and then cut each slice into quarters. Shred ginger. Pound peppercorns until partly crushed or bruised. Crumble the stock cube and cut spring onions into 5 cm (2 in) shavings and carrots into 12 mm (½ in) slices.

Cooking
Pack half the meat at the bottom of a large heat-proof basin or pan. Sprinkle evenly with 1½ tsp salt, shredded ginger and peppercorns. Lay half the onions and all the carrots on top. Repeat by laying the remainder of the meat, potato and onion on top of the previous layers. Sprinkle again with the remainder of the salt and peppercorns. Pour in the water to cover all the ingredients. Close the top of the basin with a lid or greaseproof paper. Place the pot or basin in 7.5-9 cm (3-3½ in) of boiling water in the centre of the wok. Place a lid over the wok and keep the water inside at a simmer for 3½ hours. Open the lid and the pot (or basin). Sprinkle the top of the contents with spring onions and crumbled stock cube. Give the contents a few stirs. Close the top of both the pot and the wok. Leave to simmer for a further 15 mins.

Serving
Serve in the conventional manner, by bringing the pot or basin to the table and ladling out the contents into soup bowls for the individual diners.

'Chop Suey' or the American-Chinese Version of Irish Stew (for 4-6 people to be eaten with rice or Fried Rice)

    800 g-1 kg (2-2½ lb) mutton or stewing beef
    3 slices root-ginger
    2 large onions
    1 medium carrot
    3 sticks celery
    200 g (½ lb) white cabbage (or Chinese cabbage)
    2-3 stalks spring onion
    12 peppercorns
    2 tbs vegetable oil

2 tsp salt (or to taste)
875 ml (1¾ pints) water
1½ chicken stock cubes

Preparation
Cut meat into thick 2.5 cm × 4 cm (1 in × 1½ in) slices.
Shred ginger. Cut onions into thin slices, carrot and celery
slantwise into 4 cm (1½ in) sections. Cut cabbage into
2.5 cm (1 in) sections and spring onions into 2.5 cm (1 in)
sections. Pound peppercorns a few times in a mortar or
with the back of the chopper.

Cooking
Heat oil in the wok. Add meat and root-ginger and salt.
Stir-fry them together over high heat for 4-5 mins. Add
onions and carrots and pour in 500 ml (1 pint) of the water.
Bring to boil and simmer gently for 1¼ hours under cover.
Add celery and cabbage and remainder of the water. Bring
to boil and simmer gently for 30 mins. Sprinkle with
crumbled stock cubes and spring onion, stir and cook
gently for a further 15 mins.

Serving
Serve in a large bowl or tureen for the diners to help
themselves. The dish is Chinese only in so far as it is
excellent to consume with quantities of rice.

Steak and Kidney Pudding *(for 4 people)*

600-800 g (1½-2 lb) stewing steak
200 g (½ lb) ox kidney
200 g (½ lb) button mushrooms
4 medium Chinese dried mushrooms
1 medium onion
2 tbs vegetable oil
1 tsp salt
pepper (to taste)
2 tbs soya sauce
125 ml (¼ pint) beef stock

125 ml (¼ pint) red wine
For Crust
200 g (½ lb) plain flour
1½ tsp baking powder
100 g (¼ lb) suet
2 tbs breadcrumbs
½ tsp salt
5-6 tbs water

Preparation
Make the dough by blending the ingredients for the crust together in a basin. Roll ¾ of it into a 12 mm (¼ in) thick sheet. Grease a 1 litre (2 pint) heat-proof dish or pudding basin and line it with the dough, allowing a little of it to hang over the top rim. Roll the remaining ¼ of the dough into a disc large enough to cover the top of the basin or dish. Chop steak and kidney into 2.5 cm (1 lb) pieces, cut button mushrooms into thick slices (including stalk). Soak Chinese mushrooms in water for 30 mins, remove stalks and cut caps into quarters. Slice onions.

Cooking and Serving
Heat oil in the wok. Add steak and kidney, mushrooms, onion, salt and pepper. Stir-fry over high heat for 4-5 mins. Add soya sauce, stock, wine, spring onion and ginger. Stir until the contents boil. Allow them to simmer for 5 mins. Pour the contents into the heat-proof basin or pudding basin which has been lined with dough-sheet. Close the top with the separate dough disc and trim off any excess edges. Place and tie a round piece of greaseproof paper over the top.

Bring about 7.5-9 cm (3-3½ in) depth of water to boil in the wok. Place the pudding basin or heat-proof dish in the centre of the wok (if a heat-proof dish is used it will have to be placed on top of a rack or cake tin). Place a lid firmly over the wok. Keep the water in the wok at a simmer for

3½-4 hours, when the pudding should be ready to serve.
Serve in the conventional way.

Lancashire (or Bolton) Hot-Pot *(for 4-6 people)*

  1.25 kg (3 lb) neck of lamb
  2 medium onions
  3 slices root-ginger
  3 lamb's kidneys
  12 oysters (or large mussels)
  800 g (2 lb) potatoes
  1 chicken stock cube
  3 tbs vegetable oil
  salt and pepper (to taste)
  1½ tsp sugar
  1½ tbs plain flour
  750 ml (1½ pints) good stock
  1½ tbs lard
  8 large button mushrooms
  1½ tbs soya sauce

Preparation
Cut meat into 4 cm (1½ in) pieces and onions into slices.
Shred ginger. After removing membrane and gristle, cut
each kidney into 4 slices and each slice into halves. Cut
each mushroom into quarters. Blanch or parboil oysters
or mussels in 250 ml (½ pint) of boiling water for 3 mins.
Remove shells and retain half the water. Peel potatoes and
cut into thick slices. Crumble the stock cube.

Cooking
Heat oil in a large wok. When hot, add the meat and
sprinkle with salt, pepper and sugar. Brown it slightly by
turning it in the oil for 5-6 mins. Remove the meat with a
perforated spoon. Add onions and ginger and stir-fry them
for 2 mins. Sprinkle with flour and continue to stir-fry for

2 mins. Return the meat to the wok to turn a few times with the onion and ginger. Place the potatoes evenly on top of the meat. Sprinkle contents with stock cube. Pour in 500 ml (1 pint) of the stock. Bring to the boil, reduce heat to very low and leave to simmer for 1 hour under cover.

Heat lard in a frying-pan or another wok. When hot, add kidney and mushrooms. Stir-fry them over high heat for 2 mins. Add oysters (or mussels) and soya sauce. Stir-fry them together for 2 mins. Add the remainder of the stock and oyster water. Bring them to the boil. Stir and turn the contents around a few times. Pour the contents evenly over the potato and meat in the larger wok. Replace the lid and leave contents to simmer gently for another 30 mins. Pour the contents into a large heat-proof dish (or pot). Insert the dish or pot into a pre-heated oven at 190°C (370°F) gas mark 5. Leave to cook uncovered for 45 mins.

Serving
Serve by bringing the pot or dish to the table, and serve in the conventional manner by ladling out the contents of the hot-pot onto individual plates.

Pot-au-Feu (for 5-6 people)

    1 kg (2½ lb) shin of beef
    2 pairs of chicken giblets
    800 g (2 lb) beef bone (cracked)
    2 stalks of leeks
    2 medium onions
    2 medium carrots
    2 sticks celery
    3 slices root-ginger
    3 tsp salt
    2 tbs soya sauce
    3 tsp sesame oil
    1 chicken stock cube

Preparation
Cut beef into 8 large pieces and each giblet into halves. Cut all the vegetables into thick slices. Bring a large pan of water to boil. Add the meat ingredients and bones to boil for 5 mins. Drain and add them into a large heat-proof basin or pan together with all the vegetables, salt and ginger.

Cooking
Place the pan or basin in the centre of the wok to stand in 9-10 cm (3½-4 in) water. Bring the water to the boil, place a lid over the wok and cook steadily for 5-6 hours (replenishing water when necessary).

Serving
Remove the beef, beef bones, and giblets from the pot and serve them separately after dousing them with a proportion of the soya sauce mixed with sesame oil (this should greatly improve the appeal of the meat). Skim the soup of fat and add stock cube. As soon as the latter has melted, serve the soup in bowls to be eaten with meat (and rice as we do in China, but in China we would have added fresh vegetables into the soup – such as watercress, lettuce, Chinese cabbage etc. for a moment's boiling together before serving).

Chicken à la King *(the short way) (for 5-6 people)*

    1 medium chicken
    100 g (¼ lb) mushrooms
    1 medium onion
    2 small carrots
    3 tbs sliced sweet pepper
    2 tsp salt
    1½ tbs cornflour
    1 egg white
    1 egg yolk

125 ml (¼ pint) double cream
3 tbs milk
2 tbs vegetable oil
2 slices root-ginger
125 ml (¼ pint) chicken stock
1 chicken stock cube
pepper (to taste)
2 tbs dry sherry
1½ tbs chopped parsley

Preparation
Bone the chicken and cut into 4 cm × 5 cm (1½ in × 2 in) pieces. Cut mushrooms, onion, carrots and pepper into thin slices. Rub chicken pieces with salt, half the cornflour and wet with egg white. Blend yolk with cream until consistent. Blend remaining cornflour with milk.

Cooking and Serving
Heat oil in the wok. Add onion, carrots and ginger. Stir them in the oil for 3-4 mins. Pour in the stock, add the crumbled stock cube and pepper. Bring to the boil, add chicken and turn them with the other ingredients in the wok for 2 mins. Add blended cornflour. Stir in the blended yolk and cream and add sherry. Turn and stir slowly for 2 mins. Sprinkle with parsley. Serve in the conventional manner. Total time required for cooking approximately 8 mins.

Chicken à la King *(the long way) (for 5-6 people)*

1 chicken carcass
3 slices root-ginger
1-1.5 kg (2½-3½ lb) chicken
1½ tsp salt
pepper to taste
1 medium onion

2 medium carrots
1 green and 1 red pepper
100 g (¼ lb) mushrooms
1 bouquet garni
1 chicken stock cube
125 ml (¼ pint) stock
1 egg yolk
125 ml (¼ pint) double cream
2 tbs dry sherry
1½ tbs chopped parsley

Preparation
Make stock by boiling carcass in 750 ml (1½ pints) of water
with ginger until liquid is reduced by two-thirds. Bone the
chicken and chop into 4-5 cm (1½-2 in) pieces. Sprinkle
with salt and pepper to season. Cut onion and carrots into
6 mm (¼ in) slices and pepper into 12 mm (½ in) slices.
Blanch the carrots in boiling water for 3 mins and drain.

Cooking
Pack the carrots and onion at the bottom of a heat-proof
basin. Lay the chicken on top and cover with peppers and
mushrooms. Add bouquet garni. Sprinkle with crumbled
stock cube and pour in the stock. Place the basin on a rack
at the centre of the wok to stand over 9-10 cm (3½-4 in) of
water. Cover the top of dish with tin foil. Bring water to the
boil and simmer steadily for 1¼-1½ hours. Remove the
bouquet garni. Mix the egg yolk and cream until consistent
and stir the mixture into the contents of the heat-proof
dish. Cook gently for a further 10 mins.

Serving
Ten minutes before serving, sprinkle the contents with
sherry and chopped parsley. Serve in the conventional
manner.

Soya-braised Chicken with Chestnuts *(for 4-5 people)*

200g (½lb) chestnuts
1.25-1.5 kg (3.3½ lb) chicken
2 slices root-ginger
1 tsp sugar
⅔ tbs cornflour
250 ml (½ pint) good stock
3 tbs vegetable oil
salt to taste
4 tbs soya sauce
1 chicken stock cube
4 tbs dry sherry

Preparation
Shell the chestnuts after blanching in boiling water for 2-4 mins. Quarter the chicken and cut each quarter in halves and the body into quarters. Shred and mince the ginger. Blend the cornflour with a quarter of the stock.

Cooking
Heat oil in a wok. When hot, add the chicken pieces, salt, ginger, sugar and the chestnuts and stir and turn them together over high heat for 5-6 mins. Add the soya sauce and the remaining stock. Bring to the boil, place a lid over the wok and leave to simmer for 15 mins. Open the lid, add crumbled stock cube and blended cornflour. Stir and turn the contents together for 2 mins. Add sherry. Turn a few more times and the dish is ready to serve.

Serving
Serve to be eaten with boiled potatoes, plain boiled rice or Fried Rice.

Orange and Lemon Pudding *(for 6-7 people)*

1 tsp baking powder

250 g (10 oz) self-raising flour
125 g (5 oz) beef suet
6-7 tbs milk
6-7 tbs water
5 tbs salted butter
1 medium orange
1 medium lemon
5 tbs brown sugar

Preparation

Mix baking powder, flour, suet, milk and water into a soft dough. Roll it into a large round sheet (about 35 cm (14 in) in diameter). Line a large pudding basin with it after greasing the basin. Trim off the edges of the lining and roll them into a dough-lid to cover the top of the pudding when it has been stuffed. Chop the butter into small pieces. Clean and cut both the orange and lemon horizontally into halves and then the halves into 6 segments each. Place the orange and lemon pieces in a basin and mix them with the butter and sugar. Spoon the mixture into the lined basin and cover the top with the dough disc. Fold a tin foil lid over the top securely (tie with string if necessary).

Cooking and Serving

Place the pudding basin in the centre of the wok standing in about 7.5-9 cm (3-3½ in) of water. Bring the water to the boil and place a lid over the wok. Allow the pudding to simmer for at least 3 hours, replenishing the boiling water in the wok whenever necessary. Serve in the conventional manner. This is another case where the wok is used as a double-boiler as it is often used in China.

Rice Pudding *(for 4-6 people)*

100-125 g (4-5 oz) pudding rice (or glutinous rice)
3 tbs mixed dried fruits
3-4 tbs sugar

½ tsp cinnamon
1½ tbs butter
750 ml (1½ pints) milk

Preparation
Wash the rice.

Cooking and Serving
Mix all the ingredients together in a pudding basin. Close
the top of the basin with tin foil. Place the basin in the
centre of the wok to stand in 7.5-9 cm (3-3½ in) of water.
Bring water to the boil and keep it at a simmer for 2-2½
hours (replenish the water in the wok before the level is
reduced to half). Lift the tin foil, sprinkle the top of the
pudding with a little cinnamon and serve in the conventional manner.

Index

Cooking for good health books – in paperback from Grafton Books

Kenneth Lo

Cooking and Eating the Chinese Way	£1.95	☐
The Wok Cookbook	£1.95	☐
More Wok Cookery	£1.95	☐

L D Michaels

The Complete Book of Pressure Cooking	£1.95	☐

Franny Singer

The Slow Crock Cookbook	£1.95	☐

Janet Walker

Vegetarian Cookery	£2.50	☐

David Scott

The Japanese Cookbook	£1.95	☐

Marika Hanbury Tenison

Cooking with Vegetables (illustrated)	£1.95	☐
Deep-Freeze Cookery	£1.95	☐

Pamela Westland

Low-Fat Cookery	£2.95	☐
Bean Feast	£2.50	☐
High-Fibre Vegetarian Cookery	£2.50	☐
The Complete Grill Cookbook	£1.50	☐

David Canter, Kay Canter and Daphne Swann

The Cranks Recipe Book (illustrated)	£3.95	☐

To order direct from the publisher just tick the titles you want and fill in the order form.

HB381

All these books are available at your local bookshop or newsagent, or can be ordered direct from the publisher.

To order direct from the publishers just tick the titles you want and fill in the form below.

Name _____

Address _____

Send to:
Grafton Cash Sales
PO Box 11, Falmouth, Cornwall TR10 9EN.

Please enclose remittance to the value of the cover price plus:

UK 60p for the first book, 25p for the second book plus 15p per copy for each additional book ordered to a maximum charge of £1.90.

BFPO 60p for the first book, 25p for the second book plus 15p per copy for the next 7 books, thereafter 9p per book.

Overseas including Eire £1.25 for the first book, 75p for second book and 28p for each additional book.

Grafton Books reserve the right to show new retail prices on covers, which may differ from those previously advertised in the text or elsewhere.